CW01091517

Stirring rugby tales
of the glorious
Third Fifteen...
on and off the pitch.

~ featuring ~

The Prof.

Billy
Oddsocks

Double
Dick

Jessie

d'Arcy Orders

Cover illustration by Colin King

First published in Great Britain by Pen Press

All paper used in the printing of this book has been made from
wood grown in managed, sustainable forests.

ISBN 978-1-78003-299-3

Printed and bound in the UK

Pen Press is an imprint of
Indepenpress Publishing Limited
25 Eastern Place
Brighton
BN2 1GJ

A catalogue record of this book is available from
the British Library

AUTHOR'S ACKNOWLEDGEMENTS

My thanks are due to:

Valerie-Anne and Colin King who suggested the title
and provided encouragement...

Vivienne Hall who introduced me to the art of
punctuation...

Susie, my beloved wife, who spent many solitary evenings
working on her needlepoint...

Colin King for designing the eye-catching cover...

Lynn Ashman and her talented team at Pen Press...

Of those copies printed the first fifty have been numbered
one to fifty; this copy is numbered .....**42**.

d'Arcy Orders

Cambridge
October 2011

NICE TRY

STIRRING TALES OF THE 3RD XV, BILLYODDSOCKS,
DOUBLEDICK AND THE PROF, NOT FORGETTING
JESSIE (34D cup)

These tales would n'er be
told but
an idle fellow such as I done writ them down
(attributed to Rudling Kipyard)

compiled by d'Arcy Orders

Characters

Peter Grant	'The Prof' – erudite windbag
Jessie Grant	Peter's sister; subject of fantasies (some quite rude) of rugby club and tea-lady extraordinaire
William Stephens	'Billyoddsocks' – all-time great wing forward in his twilight years
Richard Richards	'Doubledick' – legendary 3rd XV scrum-half and husband of Jessie
Charles Brown	'Beebie' – official linesman of 3rd XV
James Lambert	Dropper of passes and opera convert
John Flower	'Colly' – failed events organiser
Robert Sharp	'Raz' – serious expert on the horses
John Smith	Oath-uttering specialist
Tony Reynolds	WWI hero (MC) and pre-war captain of 3rd XV
Gerald Watson	Ardent suitor of Esmerelda
Egerton L Johnson	'Eggie' – rugby club bard

Contents

PROLOGUE

It was said that the rugby club had existed since time immemorial, although some of the older members claimed that it had been three years before that. There was a legend that the club had been formed in early Victorian times for football players. The evidence for this was a letter by a sailor in Nelson's navy sent in the 1800s from Alexandria to his family in the village; he wrote, '*We sometimes go ashore and kick a ball about and score goals like we used to on Jackson's Piece.*' Jackson's Piece was the land in the village adjacent to St George's Church. In the 1930s, two senior members of the rugby club vouched for the existence of this letter, which they claimed to have seen in the late 1890s. Unfortunately, the letter, together with the rugby club's memorabilia, was destroyed by a disastrous fire in 1900 during a party to celebrate the relief of Ladysmith. The fire was caused by a member letting off some rockets up the chimney of the front room of the honorary secretary's thatched cottage where the club's records were then stored.

Overlooking one end of the pitch was St George's, which was a typical eighteenth-century village church topped with a crenulated roof and a sturdy square tower decorated with an elegantly carved pinnacle in each corner. On the side of the tower facing the pitch was a large clock which, traditionally, was used for timing matches.

Close to the other side of the pitch was the Rose & Crown, which had always played a vital role in the life of the rugby club. It was an ancient rambling building of indeterminate age with one bar. Behind the counter was a

1

wide arch, and visible down four steps was a row of seven barrels from which all beers were drawn personally by the landlord. The only foods available were hard-boiled eggs floating in a sinister-looking off-white liquid in a glass jar plus packets of Smith's crisps.

Because of the limited size of the bar in the Rose & Crown, a previous landlord had permitted the rugby club to convert the two barns adjacent to the Rose & Crown to provide a rugby club bar, changing rooms and other facilities. An internal communicating door to the bar of the Rose & Crown enabled supporters in the rugby club area, whilst watching a match through the large windows, to luxuriate in a steady flow of alcoholic beverages from the Rose & Crown at the same time as enjoying a certain amount of privacy in a comfortable ambience. The rugby club bar in the barn was small and cosy. The two sides at right angles to the bar counter were lined with bench seating, the walls above covered with fading photographs of great English rugby teams of the 1920s and 1930s and a few past club 1st XVs, plus one picture of the legendary 3rd XV which in one memorable season, 1922–23, won more games than it lost.

The majority of the members of the rugby club were born in the village, school friends or sons of members or related by marriage. Although the rugby club in the nearby town played a higher standard of rugby, rarely would a village member choose to change clubs. If he did, he would feel excluded from the social life of the village and the stigma would remain attached to him for the rest of his life. Such a defection would be accepted only if it were obvious that the player was sufficiently talented to go on to play representative rugby.

The fixture list did not vary materially from season to season; the same 12 teams were played twice each season, home and away.

As in most sporting clubs, Saturdays were extremely busy. Soon after noon, if playing at home, members of the 3rd XV were the first to arrive in order to have sufficient time to finalise their Machiavellian tactics intended to ensure the defeat of that afternoon's opponents; also, they considered it prudent to sink a beer or two to avoid any risk of dehydration during the match.

The bar opened soon after tea and licensing hours became a distant memory. From nine o'clock there was a steady exodus to the village dance, leaving a hard core of non-dancers who lingered until the barman refused to serve them any more   drinks.

The following chapters are an attempt, before the sunset fades, to record the activities in the 1930s, both on and off the pitch, of members of a rugby 3rd XV.

THE THIRD XV

The 3rd XV was a tight-knit group of gentlemen (to use the word loosely) who, every Saturday afternoon, gave their all (or what was left of it after the customary Friday evening's festivities) for the honour and glory of the 3rd XV. It was difficult to become part of the team, but once a player had been selected – and subsequently approved by the 3rd XV regulars – he became a member, virtually for life. Rather like the Masons; the latter have their aprons and funny signs and the 3rd XV had their jock-straps and signs, although most of the 3rd XV signs might be considered somewhat vulgar. There was no question of being selected; if an accepted member of the 3rd XV wished to play and was physically fit to do so, he played. Some unkind critics (usually someone not selected) claimed that some of the 3rd XV were only just physically capable of playing. Nevertheless they exercised their inalienable right to play acquired through long – and really long – service to the 3rd XV. If a 3rd XV player did not realise that the end of his playing days was approaching too closely for comfort, the rest of the team dropped enough hints to alert him.

For many years it had been the custom for anyone wishing to join the rugby club to be invited to play his first game in the 3rd XV, the members of which were considered to be shrewd judges of human character and well able to assess the applicant's rugby skills. Also, more importantly, to decide whether he was 'the right sort of chap'.

Only on one occasion did the 3rd XV make what turned out to be a wrong decision.

A newly appointed curate from a local church applied for membership. Opinion of his suitability was divided. Billyoddsocks was strongly in favour of accepting him on the grounds that the leader of the curate's religion knew how to turn water into wine, just the sort of person to be a member of the bar committee. The curate was invited to play the following week. He was a competent player by 3rd XV standards, but after the match he insisted on wearing his dog-collar in the bar. This had an inhibiting effect on those present, who felt that they were obliged to choose their adjectives with greater care and, generally, behave in a manner suitable for being in the presence of a member of the cloth.

The matter came to a head at the next training session. Fred Green said, forcefully, 'As you all know, I am a policeman. Do I turn up in the bar wearing a policeman's helmet?'

Doubledick turned to the rest of us, asking, 'Does Fred turn up wearing a policeman's helmet?'

There were murmured replies: 'I've never noticed.' 'I'm not sure.' 'What does a policeman's helmet look like?'

Fred, irritated at not being taken seriously, continued, 'No, I do not. And why don't I? Because I am off duty. He's off duty as well, so he shouldn't wear his dog-collar.'

Fortunately, no action became necessary because, soon after the discussion, the curate announced that he was no longer available, no doubt because he realised that the rugby club in general and the 3rd XV in particular were an evangelical challenge too far.

The 3rd XV was built around an experienced hard core of about ten senior members who 15 or 20 years before had been the stars of the 1st XV until the ravages of wine, women and song (not so much the song) had necessitated their relegation to the 3rd XV. There they tenaciously went through the motions of playing rugby, using all the cunning and guile accumulated over the years with a loose interpretation of the rules, particularly those relating to offside.

The remainder of the team was made up with relatively young players who showed promise and had ambitions to be selected for the 1st XV. These were expected to do most of the running about.

It should not be thought that the 3rd XV failed to take their rugby seriously. On Monday evenings there was a Selection Committee meeting preceded by training (running round the ground a few times). Unfortunately, several of the senior members, because of business and other commitments (or so they claimed), were able to arrive only in time for the post-training beers. Thursday evenings meant more circuits of the ground and were a must. These two evenings of rigorous training were necessary to keep the 3rd XV in peak condition.

Before the match on Saturdays, the 3rd XV met at half past twelve to plan strategy and tactics. The meeting was held in the bar, where a few beers would be consumed. Playing almost the same teams twice each season, home and away, the 3rd XV and a large proportion of the members of the opposing teams knew each other from previous fixtures. When the opponents arrived, there would be welcoming beers all round to celebrate meeting old friends.

The pattern of most of the 3rd XV matches was the same. Fuelled by the pre-match beers and full of pent-up nervous energy, the 3rd XV would dominate the first half and build up a lead; 20 points was considered to be the minimum required.

Then, as the nervous energy was expended and the lunchtime beer brought on a marked lethargy, the match became a grim defensive battle, with the 3rd XV needing to defend their lead to gain a victory because they rarely scored in the second half.

There was one exception to this pattern.

One Saturday lunchtime, during the pre-match game plan discussions, a lady came into the club bar carrying two large baskets of Victoria plums. She asked if someone would be so kind as to deliver them to Jessie, the tea-lady, who, she understood, had offered to make jam to raise funds for the club.

The sight of these fat, luscious Victoria plums, obviously freshly picked, was too much for the 3rd XV. The plums began disappearing between pints of ale. It was discovered that the removal of a few plums could be concealed by shaking the baskets, but, as time passed, the reduction in the contents gradually became all too apparent.

The Prof, characteristically foreseeing problems, intervened, saying in his succinct way, 'It would seem to me, and I do not want any of you here to think or even suspect that what I am about to say should be taken as a suggestion that any of us here present has indulged in any act which could be considered, or, I might say, could be *construed*,' (the Prof repeated this word, really savouring the two syllables of what, it was suspected, was a word new to him), 'yes, construed by its nature as bordering on, for the sake of a better word, criminality. But it seems to me that Jessie is unlikely to be aware of the number of baskets of plums delivered for her kind self, so we need not further waste our time rearranging the plums but merely empty one basket into the other, conceal the superfluous basket and hope for the best.'

Clever chap, the Prof, possessing a brain way ahead of the average 3rd XV forward.

The 3rd XV took to the field to do battle against their deadly local rivals from the next village. Well into the second half, the 3rd XV realised that they had not established their minimum first-half lead of 20 points and were in fact trailing 21–15.

Because the digestive systems of the members of the 3rd XV were somewhat more delicate and sensitive than those of the average rugby player, and aggravated by the effect of an unfamiliar intake of fat, luscious, freshly-picked Victoria plums, mingling with the quantities of ale consumed, the resulting potent mixture began to make its presence felt.

Most people are aware of the purgative effect of fresh fruit, and the quantity consumed by the 3rd XV produced acute results, which made the usual remedial action imperative and urgent if a rather unpleasant and embarrassing predicament was to be avoided. The only hope of salvation was a quick visit to the pavilion, but the 3rd XV's opponents were defending the pavilion end and the 3rd XV rarely, in the second half, spent any time in their opponents' half of the pitch. This was an emergency.

Suddenly, immense pressure built up in the 3rd XV scrum, the forwards sweeping up the field, scoring a try in the corner nearest the pavilion. Immediately, three figures detached themselves from the mass of players and made a dash for the pavilion, shouting to the scrum-half as he was collecting the ball for the conversion kick, 'Take your time, Sam.' They returned, somewhat shamefacedly, a few minutes later, in time for the restart of play.

This ploy was of necessity repeated two or three times, during which the 3rd XV managed to score a second try, enabling them to scrape a draw.

Jessie, having collected jam jars, lids and labels to produce a large quantity of plum jam, was puzzled and a little disappointed when only half the jars she had prepared were filled.

THE PROF AND THE VILLAGE MAGAZINE

Soon after joining the rugby club, the Prof acquired his nickname following an informal discussion with 3rd XV members in the club bar about the aims and thinking process of a successful rugby team. His contribution was, 'What a good rugby team needs is an integrated, parallel mobility plus a responsive, reciprocal approach; these concepts may not appear to you to be compatible, but that is the only way a team can guarantee synchronised flexibility and, it follows, success.'

All those included in the discussion were dumb-struck, although someone at the back was heard to say, 'I don't know what he says, but don't 'e talk lovely?'

From then on, Peter Grant became affectionately known as 'the Prof', his future pronouncements being tolerated because, long-winded though they were, they usually contained a view relevant to the subject under discussion

The Prof, whilst he considered himself a member of the 3rd XV, was not a particularly regular player; most of his friends were, and they enjoyed listening to his lengthy and pompous statements. In any case, he was the brother of Jessie, and if anyone desired to make any progress in Jessie's affections it was felt to be a sensible policy to keep on the right side of the Prof. He was always available if a player dropped out and absolutely no replacement could be found, so he would make up the numbers of the 3rd XV. He used to say that his value to the club was that although his rugby skills were strictly limited, he could play inadequately in any position, except full-back; in that position he was a first-class coward.

The Prof was tall, lanky and sometimes awkward in movement. His very dark hair surmounted black-rimmed spectacles, and the bow tie which he invariably wore with a suit purchased, he proudly stated, from 'Burton's, the 50-bob tailors' gave him an elegant, if foppish appearance.

The village enjoyed the luxury of a village magazine, founded and financed by an enthusiastic but eccentric honorary editor. It was produced with the help of volunteers and a part-time, salaried typist. Financially, the magazine continually struggled to break even. Its presentation was somewhat flamboyant, and for short periods its appearance on the bookstalls was, to say the least, spasmodic.

The Prof had not been known for his academic ability at the village school with which he had recently, by mutual consent, parted company, mainly because his thoughts had not been occupied with school work but with his two burning ambitions, becoming a journalist and a crime writer.

The Prof's first attempt at journalism was whilst still at school; in Form 4B, he produced the six-page 4B News at tuppence per copy. The main features were a series of short, 30–40-word biographies of masters and their idiosyncrasies, all amusing and in no way offensive.

News of the Prof's intentions reached the staff and he was alarmed when he was summoned by the deputy head, fearing the worst.

'Ah, Grant, it has come to my knowledge that you are planning to produce some sort of Form 4B newsletter, what? Shows initiative, don't you see. But you'll understand that there will have to be a master to keep an eye on what you're up to. D'you follow? I have asked' (he really meant 'told') 'Mr Henson' (English master) 'to watch what you are doing, if you follow. He's the best chap for the job, d'you see?'

The Prof hadn't been required to contribute a word to the interview and was greatly relieved to learn that he had official editorial clearance.

He duly cobbled together six pages of editorial, including the masters' biographies, and then delivered the proof for approval to Mr Henson, whose immediate reaction was to tell the Prof that in no circumstances could the biographies be included, and they must be removed *in toto*. The teachers would lose the respect of the pupils; their authority would be seriously impaired.

The Prof had spent a great deal of time on writing these biographies and was proud of his work. He was furious, and swore to exact retribution from Mr Henson.

After Mr Henson approved the new sanitised version, the Prof was authorised to ask Lucy, the school secretary, to prepare a stencil and run off on the school's duplicating machine 40 copies of the Form 4B newsletter.

The main feature of the newsletter was a report of a football match between the Gentlemen of Form 4B and the Swots of Form 4A.

The final paragraph read:

...the two teams were evenly-matched and with the score two goals each and only minutes of play left, a draw seemed the most likely result. But when a 4B forward broke through and aimed a shit at goal, the goal-keeper was surprised (I suppose he would be) *and let it slip through his hands into the back of the 4A net.*

The misprint was soon noticed and the deputy head urgently wanted to know who was responsible. The Prof stated that he had clearly written 'shot' and that Mr Henson had approved the draft; Mr Henson claimed that when he had checked the draft he would have noticed the incorrect spelling and Lucy insisted she had typed only what she saw.

How the error occurred was never ascertained, although Mr Henson was suspected by the deputy head of being at fault. Personally, I feel it wouldn't be surprising if there was an element of collusion and the Prof knew more than he admitted; Lucy was very attractive and the Prof always said that he preferred the older woman.

Although the 4B newsletter never again appeared, all 40 copies were sold. It is unlikely that even Northcliffe could claim that he sold all the copies of his very first publishing venture.

To prepare himself for his desired career, that of a journalist and crime writer, the Prof took two steps: firstly to insinuate himself on to the staff of the village magazine, and secondly to read all the reports of crimes he could find, particularly the series of books *Notable British Trials* by William Roughead.

As with most journals, revenue from advertising was the life-blood of the publication. The Prof's first assignment was a test of his suitability. He was to obtain, on a small commission basis, advertisements from local firms. The editor's practice was to insert inexpensive, brief but informative adverts amongst the editorial columns.

The Prof set off first thing the following morning, determined to obtain advertisements from some firms suggested by the editor, and others which the Prof proposed to target. He returned just before lunch, gleefully waving his order book, exclaiming, 'I've got five ads!'

The editor read them out in front of the staff. They were:

J Brown & Sons, Undertakers
Our Motto – All's well that ends well

The MIRACLE Pie Company
If it tastes good, it's a MIRACLE

Lyons Corner House
If you want the best food, try our other branches

Premier Printers Ltd
Your Perfect Prunters

The Reliable Driving School
Learn to Drive Quickly – TAKE OUR CRASH COURSE

It was then that the Prof realised that he had been set up.

After a week trying to sell legitimate advertising, the Prof confided in me that he experienced great difficulty in persuading possible advertisers to sign a contract, the reason being the small circulation of the magazine, but that he had the answer to increase the sales of the magazine.

The Prof then changed the subject, asking me, 'You are my best friend, aren't you?'

'Yes, I like to think so.'

'You would do anything to help me?'

'Well, I suppose so.'

'And you have a dog, a golden cocker spaniel, what's her name, er, Gertie, I believe?'

By now, I was beginning to be suspicious about where this conversation was leading. 'What's that have to do with the magazine?'

'Well, I have been reading about newspapers and their proprietors. In one book, Lord Northcliffe states that "Dog Bites Man" is not news, but "Man Bites Dog" would be dramatic news. A spin-off would be the publicity which would greatly increase circulation.'

I said, 'So?'

'I need a photograph of a man biting a dog to put in the magazine. Before you say anything, the editor thinks it is an exciting idea. As I am your best friend and you have a dog, I thought you would be quite willing to help.'

'But the readers of the magazine would recognise me. No one would ever speak to me again. In any case, they would think it was some kind of hoax.'

'I guarantee that the man will not be recognisable. It doesn't matter what readers think; it is the publicity which is important.'

I, reluctantly, agreed

On Saturday morning, the Prof arrived with a Kodak box camera to take the photograph. As I took up my position, I remember saying, 'Sorry, Gertie, old girl, but to help my best friend, I have to bite a bit out of your backside.'

Gertie gave me a look which I interpreted as, 'Well, he is *not* my best friend.'

The Prof took a roll of film and after trying various angles took a roll-full of photographs whilst Gertie and I adopted poses he suggested. For my trouble, I received a mouthful of eight-year-old golden cocker spaniel hair.

One of the developed photographs was particularly realistic. As the Prof had promised, the man was unrecognisable and Gertie was shown looking back over her shoulder with a puzzled, long-suffering look on her lovable canine face.

It was then, to my horror, that I realised that many people in the village knew that Gertie was my dog, and would obviously put two and two together.

Too late; the mighty presses were poised ready to roll.

Within hours of the magazine being published, the editor was bombarded by emotionally charged letters and telephone calls and, several times, accosted in the street. People wanted to know what sort of man needed to resort to such a cruel act; was he an unemployed miner? Why didn't the photographer intervene and save the dog? Endless assorted complaints.

Other subscribers soon realised that the photograph was a hoax and contributed some witty remarks. A representative of the RSPCA called at the editorial office to be reassured.

The Prof was right. As a direct result of the publicity generated, sales of the next issue of the magazine, containing four extra pages of readers' letters, almost doubled. The Prof, obviously, a man to watch.

To fill the magazine, the editor initiated a series of personal interviews with the local Great and Good: their background career, interests and ambitions. These were made sufficiently flattering to, hopefully, generate much-wanted donations from the subjects of the interviews.

The first was the squire: Cambridge – Sandhurst, Boer War, huntin' and shootin'. Ambition: a younger wife.

Then the vicar – Harrow, lacrosse blue 1888; curate, Bolton. Ambition: captain of village cricket team or Archbishop of Canterbury, preferably both. Landlord of the Red Lion – army; Glasshouse, Aldershot; merchant navy. Ambition: a serious fire at the close-by Rose & Crown.

The editor suggested that people taking up residence in the village should be routinely approached for an interview. A recent arrival was a Mrs Whititstone, and because she was rarely seen in the village little was known about her and she was regarded as a mystery woman. She was now being looked after by staff who played little part in the life of the village, apart from visiting the shops. She ventured out only to attend church once each Sunday. The vicar was known to call occasionally on her, usually leaving with generous donations for the church or village good causes. The editor's plan was to ask for an interview and hope to obtain information about her past to be published, suitably edited, to satisfy the curiosity of the villagers.

By a remarkable coincidence, the Prof, during his wide reading of criminal cases, had come across the case of a Hetty Whititstone who some 25 years before had been charged with and acquitted of the murder of her lover. In a flash, the Prof realised that his journalistic career was about to begin with a bang; a scoop had dropped into his lap – if, and only if, Mrs Whititstone would agree to being interviewed. He composed an obsequious letter which he persuaded Millie, one of the staff of Mrs Whititstone whom he contrived to bump into when she was shopping in the village, to deliver to her employer. A favourable reply was received via the same courier, suggesting 4pm the following Thursday.

Triumphantly, the Prof told the village magazine editor. He was not only surprised that Mrs Whititstone had agreed to an interview but also was greatly impressed by the Prof's initiative in arranging it.

The facts of the case were: Hetty Whititstone, married to a commercial traveller, was a trained midwife who, according to the press, had been highly thought of for bringing numerous babies into the world but had lost respect all round when it appeared that she had helped someone out of it. Her husband was financially very successful in his chosen calling, and they lived in grand style in a large house with three staff: a couple in their thirties, Mary and George Morgan, and Millie, a young maidservant. Mrs Whititstone became very friendly with a retired Indian army officer, Major Western-Cole, typical in every way, with moustache, red face, check suits and walking stick. When Mr Whititstone was travelling, the major took to calling on Mrs Whititstone for formal tea and cakes once or twice per month. The tea must have been of a somewhat potent brew, because after a few cups the tea party became rather less formal and about an hour or so later the gallant major could be seen departing from the house with all the courtesies and a face three hues redder than when he had arrived, leaving Mrs Whititstone with a satisfied smile on her pretty face.

Owing to the nature of her profession of midwife, the Major would sometimes arrived to discover that his hostess was absent on her professional duties; it was difficult to determine the precise time of arrival of humans into this world. It was alleged that, in these circumstances, Mary Morgan, wishing the major to avoid a wasted journey and being of a helpful disposition, would, as it were, stand in for her mistress.

Inevitably, this magnanimous gesture, beyond the normal call of a servant's duty, would ultimately come to the knowledge of both Mary Morgan's husband and Mrs Whititstone. In addition, the latter's activities would, equally inevitably, become known to her husband.

The unsuspecting major's visits had increased because, in the new circumstances of Mary Morgan's helpful disposition, there was less chance of a wasted journey and his visits had acquired a certain piquancy, because he was never able to anticipate who would be pouring out the tea.

On his next visit, all was decorum because of the presence of Mr Whititstone at home. Tea, together with buns, was served. After a shorter than usual tea party, the major returned to his home, where he began to suffer severe abdominal pains. The doctor was summoned but arrived only in time to hear the major's last words, which must rank with Nelson's 'Kiss me, Hardy' and Charles II's 'Let not poor Nelly starve'; his words were, 'It was them buns.'

In spite of the major's grammar deserting him as he neared the pearly gates, the doctor was able to understand the possible import of those words and summoned the police. A post-mortem disclosed that the major had absorbed sufficient arsenic to despatch half a regiment, let alone one officer and gentleman.

During their routine enquiries the police searched the house and were told by Mrs Whititstone that stocks of arsenic were indeed kept in the garden shed, but solely for the purpose of killing daisies on the lawn. To prove her point, in a dramatic gesture, she stood up and flung open the French windows to expose a spacious lawn with not a daisy in sight.

All the residents of the house were suspects, including Millie, who, it was later disclosed, the major had had some sort of hold over or may have been molesting. Mary Morgan had baked the buns, but then it was established that all the suspects had had the opportunity of mixing the arsenic with the flour. Mr Morgan and Mr Whititstone could each have resented the gallant major's intimacy with their respective wives.

As the police learned that the major had left Mrs Whititstone a substantial sum of money, she was charged with the crime of murder. After a trial lasting three days, the jury concluded that as there were several suspects, each with a possible motive, there was a reasonable doubt of her guilt and she was acquitted.

On the prescribed day the Prof, attired in his reporter's natty gent's suiting, arrived at 4pm to be warmly greeted by Mrs Whititstone. A simple black dress with pearl buttons down the front and a large Victorian brooch on her left breast showed off her trim figure to advantage; her hair, beginning to grey, was swept back into a bun. It was obvious that she had been and still was, 25 years later, very attractive.

Tea was brought in but, despite Mrs Whititstone being friendly and loquacious, as the time passed the Prof gradually lost his nerve, became tongue-tied and couldn't bring himself to ask questions about the murder, the real purpose of his visit. It was later, when the housekeeper brought in a plate of buns, which Mrs Whititstone offered the Prof with the words, 'I think you will like these; I've been using the recipe for years and it has always worked,' that the Prof's resolve entirely cracked. The remaining time was spent in trivial conversation.

As the Prof was leaving, Mrs Whititstone took him by the arm and said, 'I do hope you have obtained all the information you require for the village magazine. I had expected you to ask me whether I am the Mrs Whititstone in the murder case; most people do ask me, you know. It is such an unusual name.' She shook the Prof's hand and said, 'Goodbye.'

When the Prof returned to the magazine office, he realised that his notebook was almost bare. The editor was not best pleased and asked, 'Well, is she the notorious Hetty Whititstone?' to which the Prof could only reply, lamely, 'She didn't say.'

In journalistic terms, the Prof had 'blown' his first scoop.

Demobbed from the army in 1946, the Prof emigrated to the United States, becoming editor of a large provincial newspaper. None of his rugby club contemporaries could visualise the Prof in shirt sleeves, wearing a green eye-shade and rushing through the editorial room, clutching a sheaf of papers, shouting, 'Hold the front page!'

BILLYODDSOCKS: THE THINKING MAN'S RUGBY PLAYER

One of the legendary characters of the rugby club was William Stevens. After he arrived at school wearing odd socks he became affectionately known as Billyoddsocks, a nickname which stayed with him for the rest of his life.

Some unkind critics alleged that Billy, having left school, had applied to join the rugby club and been invited to play fly-half for the 1st XV, but, following his first appearance, had been selected on merit for the 3rd XV.

Billy explained his presence in that team by a rather touching story of how he had, unselfishly, shunned a remarkable rugby career and a possible England cap 'to show the young lads how to play rugby properly', whatever that meant.

Billy may not have been the best player of the 3rd XV but he was, by far, the best dressed. Every Saturday he turned up to play clad in a spotless shirt and shorts, wearing well-polished boots. To say that he was immaculate would be an understatement, except for the fact that his socks were usually spilling over his boots. This discordant element in his appearance led to much discussion of possible reasons for what appeared to be a deliberate practice.

As no one had actually asked Billy for an explanation, Doubledick and I were deputed to take up the matter with

Billy. After a few pleasantries, the following conversation with Billy took place:

'Billy, you are generally regarded as the best-dressed member of the 3rd XV,' (the bit about his not being the best player was omitted), 'but why do you turn up to play with your socks spilling all over your boots?'

Billy's reply was, 'I am glad you asked me that question. As you are aware, as a rugby player, I am very energetic and industrious, if that is the appropriate expression, and I do a great deal of running about...'

Doubledick interjected, 'And sometimes you have the ball with you.'

Ignoring this unkind remark, Billy continued, 'If I wear club socks, I will need elastic bands to keep them in place; I am concerned that the resulting pressure on my arteries might deprive my legs of the required amount of blood, because, to transport my 14 stone' (Billy's optimistic estimate) 'round the rugby field at a reasonable pace, my legs need all the blood that they can get.'

There was no doubting that Billy did a lot of running about. He could always be seen trundling along behind the main body of forwards. When there was a set scrum, Billy would arrive just in time to lean on the back of a second-row forward to regain his breath, packing down in his position as wing-forward seconds before the scrum broke up.

Billy's plausible explanation was accepted by the interested members.

Despite his playing career being confined to the 3rd XV, first as fly-half and later as wing-forward, Billy became a larger than life character – 25lbs larger, actually – and was generally regarded as the thinking man's rugby player, applying his mighty intellect to solving the 3rd XV's tactical problems, the most urgent of which was the procedure to be followed after the 3rd XV forwards had heeled the ball. Usually, the scrum-half passed the ball to the fly-half for onward transmission, via the three-quarters, to the wing, who was expected to make a resolute dash for the opponent's try-line. Because the 3rd XV backs were not particularly dexterous and their passes were chancy, by the time the ball reached the 3rd XV wing, he would be confronted by a phalanx of defenders and promptly tackled in possession.

Billy's solution was this: when the ball reached the fly-half he would, with a deft kick, lob the ball over the heads of the approaching defenders. Because of the unpredictable bounce of rugby balls, the 3rd XV wing speeding towards the ball might have the opportunity of gathering the ball and sprinting to the opponents' line. Provided the wing was not busy chatting up his girlfriend on the touchline, this tactic often led to a try.

Billy realised that the success of this ploy would be greater if the wing could be alerted by the fly-half of his intention. He therefore devised a cunning signal. The fly-half would ostentatiously take out a white handkerchief from the pocket of his shorts and blow his nose. Recognising the signal, the wing-three-quarter would begin galloping towards where he anticipated the ball would land.

This tactic did improve the success rate until the match when the fly-half turned up suffering from a streaming cold. Every time he blew his nose, the wing could be seen racing down the touchline for no apparent reason, whilst play continued in another part of the pitch.

Billy's long sojourn in the 3rd XV and his increasing patriarchal gravitas did give him a certain amount of authority and prestige, so when he promoted his other contribution, the theory of corner-flagging, he received full attention.

Basically, if the 3rd XV opponents were attacking down their right, Billy, as wing-forward, would launch himself from a scrum in a straight line in the direction of the threatened right hand corner. Billy's theory was: 'If

Archimedes and Pythagoras are to be taken seriously, to get to our try-line, any attacker must, repeat, must cross the line of my trajectory, where I can nab him.'

However, it appeared that because the two Greeks had not played a great deal of rugby, they lacked knowledge of the finer points of the game. Billy would either pass some way behind the attacker or a yard in front. This conduct, whilst it puzzled the attacking player, did not weaken his resolve to place the ball over the 3rd XV's try-line.

When someone had the temerity to ask Billy, 'Why, if, as you say, your system is fool-proof, do the 3rd XV opponents score so many tries?' all those present noticed Billy wince at such a below-the-belt question. His reply, delivered in a manner calculated to put an end to any further discussion, was, 'In my day three-quarters ran straight'

Billy claimed that his theory was proven when he brought off a spectacular tackle, saving the 3rd XV from imminent defeat. Billy launched himself from the scrum and brought the attacker crashing to the ground.

In the bar after the match Billy was congratulated by both teams. After a few pints loosened his tongue he was honest enough to explain that things were not quite what they seemed to be. The facts were: for the umpteenth time he had 'corner-flagged', but he had suddenly been so overcome by a combination of the exertions of the afternoon and the cumulative effects of the rugby club dinner dance the previous evening that he had come over faint and collided with the three-quarter, grabbing him to break his fall and, inadvertently, bringing off what appeared to be a magnificent tackle.

Although Billy attended the Thursday evening training sessions, his attitude towards training was ambivalent. In his view, rugby was about two teams of 15 individuals who, on a Saturday afternoon, enjoyed playing a hard-fought game of rugby for 80 minutes and then adjourned to the bar to socialise over a beer or two. Training, to Billy, seemed, somehow, to be tantamount to cheating.

The way Billy spoke, the listener would gain the impression that the 3rd XV were never beaten; it was just that their opponents tended to score more points than did the 3rd XV. As he said: if their opponents scored fewer points, the 3rd XV would have a better chance of winning.

After much consideration over the years, Billy came to the conclusion that the ability of rugby players varied greatly. Ensuring that matches were more competitive and closer would be an advantage.

The only solution was to introduce some form of handicapping of particularly skilful players. He acknowledged that his suggestion was not original, citing golf. He explained that a chap named Stableford had devised a generally accepted system by which two golfers of widely differing standards of ability could still enjoy a highly competitive match. He added that horse-racing was another example; jockeys were required to carry weights to equalise the load borne by the horses, ensuring that the horse winning the race was the fastest and not the one carrying the lightest jockey.

In the case of rugby, he had, as an example, suggested that a particularly sure-footed fly-half should be required to carry a pound of rice or sand in the pocket of his shorts, but had finally realised that, in wet weather, the rice might become soggy or the sand absorb rainwater and, as a result, become heavier. This would be an unfair handicap. Waterproof shorts might be the answer, but he did not think the rugby union authorities would support such a system.

For a few years, Billy continued to play his part in the 3rd XV and the life of the rugby club, but he never really got over the stuttering scrum-half incident.

This occurred when the 3rd XV were unable to find a scrum-half and, in desperation at the last minute, persuaded a lad, Peter Watts, from the local school to play.

Early in the match Peter was tackled in possession by one of the 3rd XV players, John Bailey, who was colour blind and short-sighted and who assumed that anyone he didn't recognise must be an opponent. For that reason, nervous and overwhelmed by playing in such distinguished company, Peter began to stutter.

Billy, waiting to hear the scrum-half shout which way play was going, heard only Peter's 'g-g-g-g-goin, going...' Not knowing whether it was to be left or right and impatient, he chose the wrong option and began his corner-flagging in the direction opposite to where play was actually moving, much to the amusement of the few spectators.

In the bar after the match, Billy was the subject of much teasing. He was greatly disappointed and hurt that no one believed his explanation. The incident took place on the far side of the pitch, devoid of any spectators who could corroborate him.

Billy ceased to play regularly, although he made it known that he was available in an emergency. However, 3rd XV captains preferred to play one short rather than have Billy on the side because he was liable to cost the 3rd XV 12 points in penalties for being offside.

In later years, Billy's disposition bordered on the lugubrious. He continued to provide unstinting support for the 3rd XV and contribute recommendations for team tactics, discoursing on the good old days and propounding his theories on corner-flagging. In fact, behind the rugby club bar, a pencil, paper, ruler and eraser were readily available for Billy's use to illustrate his corner-flagging theory to anyone prepared to listen and enjoy a glass of beer with him.

THE SPANISH PRINCESS

The rugby club bar was agog with the news. Not only was the local squire bringing a party to the rugby club annual dinner dance – black tie, and no dirty songs – but included in the party would be one of the squire's house guests, who was none other than a Spanish princess.

A Spanish princess. What a catch for a local lad! Think of it: a life of luxury and ease surrounded by humble servants; a passionate, well-endowed peasant girl brought up from the village every evening; a life to be sought after. Sod working for the gas company.

Billyoddsocks asked, 'Do they do the same sorts of dances we do?'

Doubledick said, 'No, definitely not the sort that are performed at the end of the rugby dinner dance. They do a lot of fandangos and that.'

Billyoddsocks asked, 'What's a fandango?'

The Prof volunteered the answer. 'As far as I know, and I cannot vouch for its accuracy, but from the information I picked up when I was attending evening classes in Spanish, a "fandango" is similar to a tango but the lady holds a fan. I suspect that the name is a corruption of the two words "fan" and "tango", hence "fandango". From my Spanish studies I could offer you other examples of similar words. One such example...'

'Head him off,' Eggie shouted across the room. The Prof had a reputation for being long-winded.

The matter was the subject of a great deal of discussion between the four of us, the Prof, Doubledick, Billyoddsocks and myself, and the following conclusions were reached:

1.   The Spanish princess spoke English. The squire was not known to speak Spanish, therefore his house guest must speak English.
2.   As the Spanish princess was attending the rugby club dinner dance, she would wish to dance, otherwise why come to the dinner dance?
3.   Although the Spanish princess might be able to dance English-style, anyone at the dinner dance who could dance the fandango would have a head start in the Spanish princess's affections.
4.   Anyone wishing to dance with the Spanish princess must learn to dance the fandango with or without holding a fan.
5.   It was obvious that fandango dancing lessons must, as a matter of urgency, be taken.

By chance, situated in a nearby village was the Leonardo Talbotti Italian Dancing School, the obvious place to make initial enquiries about fandango dancing lessons.

Some years before, Leonard Talbot had been an ardent amateur ballroom dancer, spending his evenings at various Palais de Danse, perfecting his feather steps, cross-chassis and forward-side-togethers. He and his partner had entered several amateur dancing competitions, coming second equals in the Hammersmith Palais de Danse Foxtrot Competition. The following Saturday they were again second in the Ealing Open Quick-step, and two weeks later came first in the South of England Open Foxtrot and Quick-step Championship, the last of these victories despite Leonard suffering from a slightly sprained wrist.

This remarkable run of success convinced Leonard that awaiting him was a lucrative career in the field of professional ballroom dancing. He thereupon, with remarkable originality, changed his name from Leonard Talbot to Leonardo Talbotti, rented a house with a large double sitting room on the ground floor and opened the Leonardo Talbotti Italian Dancing School.

Leonardo was a thin, sallow-complexioned man with a small black moustache on his upper lip, shiny Brylcreemed hair and a cigarette, sometimes alight, hanging from the corner of his mouth.

My enquiries at the Leonardo Talbotti Italian Dancing School revealed that the cost of a course of eight lessons would be two guineas plus ten shillings for specialist tuition in the intricacies of the fandango. This knowledge of the cost caused me a certain amount of gloom.

When I reported to my prospective colleagues, the Prof felt it necessary to make an observation, long winded as usual. 'You will forgive me if I question the wisdom in selecting an Italian, I repeat, an Italian dancing school to teach us to dance a "fandango", which is, obviously, not a dance usually associated with Italy but has, for many centuries, been particularly Spanish. Whilst I do not doubt that the achievements of Senior Talbotti in his chosen profession together with his wide experience in teaching ballroom dancing in general qualify him to share his knowledge of "fandangoing" – if you will forgive the expression – with us, will he be teaching us an "authentic" Spanish fandango? We do not wish to confuse our honoured guest, the princess, with an Italian fandango, even supposing a version of such a dance exists in Italy.'

Because I was responsible for finding and agreeing terms with Senior Talbotti, I felt it was for me to reassure the Prof, which I did. 'Prof, that is a perfectly reasonable point of view. When I called at Senor Talbotti's premises I happened to notice on a table a book entitled *Dancing the*

Fandango in Eight Easy Lessons. Should Senior Talbotti experience any doubts as to the appropriate steps required at any one time, he could readily refer to this book for guidance. You will remember that I was quoted ten shillings for additional specialist tuition in dancing a Spanish fandango.'

This appeared to satisfy the Prof, but Billyoddsocks and Doubledick began gloomily muttering their concern about the cost, two pounds 12 shillings each, a substantial sum to speculate on a rather risky investment.

I continued, 'Look, individually, none of can afford that sort of money; there are four of us interested, so the most economical arrangement would be for each of us to chip in 13 shillings, then for one of us to take the lessons and, whoever that one is, pass on what he has learned to the other three. We can use the rugby club bar when it's closed on Wednesdays to do this and practise.'

Doubledick, who could only assess the value of anything in terms of pints of beer, complained, 'Thirteen shillings each; that's nearly 20 pints of bitter.'

But who should have the lessons from Leonardo?

I said, 'The fairest way would be to cut cards. We'll meet next Tuesday and I'll bring a pack of cards.'

The next Tuesday we met for the ceremony. The cards were well shuffled and spread out on the bar counter. Billyoddsocks drew a Jack of spades, Doubledick a ten of clubs, the Prof a ten of hearts, and myself the Queen of diamonds. We hadn't used my pack of cards for nothing.

As it was me who was to take the lessons, I had to ensure that the instruction I passed on to the other three would include slight variations so as not to be exactly correct. When the great test presented itself at the rugby club dinner dance I would be the *only person* who could dance the fandango correctly, and who knew what might flow from that?

I collected the 13 shillings from each of Billyoddsocks, Doubledick and the Prof (cash up front, just to be on the safe side) and set off for the Leonardo Talbotti Italian Dancing School.

The school was somewhat lacking in Italian chic and/or style, the only Italian influence being three empty Chianti bottles standing on the piano and a coloured print of St Peter's, Rome, hanging on the wall, plus Len's occasional '*Molto bene*' and '*Arrivederci*' when a pupil arrived and sometimes when they departed. I noticed Leonardo's copy of *Dancing the Fandango in Eight Easy Lessons* lying open on top of the piano, providing me with the confidence that Leonardo had done his homework. Sometimes, to improve the ambience, he switched to '*Gracias*' and '*Muy bien*'. All Leonardo's multi-lingual greetings to create an Italian ambient were brought to nothing by the view through the large bay window, which was of miles of flat fenland with the tip of the tower of Ely Cathedral just visible on the far distant horizon.

Music was provided by dear old Flo, middle-aged, blousy and bored, who thumped out Leonardo's requirements on the upright piano, usually in E flat, at a tempo stricter than Victor Silvester ever achieved. I arrived, took to the floor and began being initiated into the secret and subtle mysteries of the fandango, or so Leonardo claimed that they were.

At first I felt ridiculous, dancing face-to-face with Len. Also, being rather exposed to Len's off-white breath and an occasional puff of smoke from the smouldering cigarette in the corner of his mouth was not exactly refreshing. Another irritant was his insistence on addressing me as 'darling'. But it was a job to be done and I had my commitment to Billyoddsocks, Doubledick and the Prof.

I began to enjoy the lessons and could visualise the Spanish princess being overcome with admiration of my nimble footwork.

The most difficult part was transferring the knowledge and skills I had acquired to Billyoddsocks, Doubledick and the Prof after my lesson each Tuesday. We met on the Wednesday evenings in the rugby club bar where, in front of the (bribed and sworn to secrecy) bar secretary, I trundled each of them in turn around the area and did my best to teach them the basic steps and actions of the fandango. It was no joke trying to steer Billyoddsocks, who weighed about 14 stone and was built like a prop forward. He treated our session like a rugby match by insisting on removing his false teeth before beginning the lesson. Because of the absence of his teeth, I could not get Billyoddsocks to reproduce that arrogant, livid expression which, I assumed, was required of male fandangoists. He just couldn't get in character.

Unfortunately, towards the end of the scheduled lessons, ugly rumours about what was going on in the barn on Wednesday evenings began to circulate and reached our ears. Some were highly imaginative and others bordering on the pornographic. All very embarrassing.

With royalty expected to be present, the required dress at the rugby club annual dinner dance was black tie for gentlemen and ball gowns for ladies. At the committee meeting at which this decision was taken, the Prof made the following proposal: 'It is well known that because of Spain being close to the equator, the inhabitants are exposed to almost continual sunshine. This has the effect of causing the busts of the Spanish ladies to develop and to become larger than average or, one could say, become voluptuous. Therefore I think that the committee would be well advised to ask Beebie's father, who, as we are all aware, occupies the office of butler at the hall, to drop a hint, diplomatically, of course, to the squire, that his royal guest should limit the depth of her cleavage to a non-provoking, respectable level because members of the rugby club are easily inflamed, particularly those members of the 3rd XV.'

There were murmurs of approval from the members of the committee. The chairman thanked the Prof profusely for his informed foresight, helping to avoid provoking what could develop into an embarrassing situation with the potential of becoming an international incident. This could, possibly, lead to diplomatic relations between England and Spain being broken off. At Beebie's request, his father duly passed on the warning to the squire's secretary.

At last the Great Day arrived. There we were, all wearing our black ties. A few minutes before supper, the buzz went round: the squire had parked his car, he was just coming in, and there he was, accompanied, arm-in-arm, by the Spanish princess. Yes, yes, she was charming, elegant and very Andalusian, but she was 70 if she was a day, and walked with the aid of a stick. Obviously, no fandangoing with a Spanish princess. We were extremely disappointed and crestfallen. All our efforts wasted and, what was more, 13 shillings (or 20 pints of beer by Doubledick's reckoning) each squandered.

The band struck up what they laughingly called a tango. All eyes turned towards the four of us. It was then that we realised that most of those present knew of our secret preparations. The girls gathered around, sarcastically beseeching each of us, with a suggestive wink, to fandango with them.

Billyoddsocks, alarmed and in a panic-stricken voice said to me, 'I've only ever danced the ladies' steps with you. You will have to dance with me.'

I replied, 'Only if you keep your teeth in.'

Doubledick and the Prof took their cue from us and we two couples danced a few laps of our version of an all-male fandango, accompanied by vulgar and, in some cases, uncouth remarks.

The performance was not authentic because only the Prof had remembered to bring a fan. He, with his impeccable logic, observed that a fandango without the fan must be a dango. When, after the event, the Prof asked me what he should do with his fan, modesty prevents me from recording what I said.

In fact, our fandango was the high spot of the evening. But, over the years, I and no doubt the others have never been allowed to forget our performance. What the Spanish princess thought of our exhibition we never knew, nor enquired, but the squire was alleged to have said, 'Well, it was an unusual spectacle, even at a rugby club social event.'

The Leonardo Talbotti Italian School of Dancing continued until the proprietor was, in 1941, called up into the army. He enlisted as Leonard Talbot, just in case he was posted to the Italian front.

THE DROPPED PASS

Over the years several apocryphal accounts concerning an unfortunate incident involving the 3rd XV have been circulating, each account embellished in the telling in the bar, and each more dramatic than that previously told.

This chapter is contributed to state, once and for all, the facts. It should be noted that names have been changed to protect the guilty.

The storybook scene: only minutes before the final whistle, the 3rd XV were trailing 15–13 in a hard-fought local derby against opponents which the 3rd XV had not beaten for 17 years.

John Smith, 15 yards from the opponents' try-line, broke through with only the opposing full-back to beat. Seconds before the full-back tackled him, he lobbed a perfect pass to unmarked Jim Lambert, who had only five unopposed yards to cover to score the winning try.

Jim Lambert dropped the ball.

The final whistle was blown, making it 18 years since the 3rd XV had been victorious against their long-time opponents. John Smith, captain of the 3rd XV, denied a historic victory and infuriated beyond reason, proceeded to direct towards Jim Lambert a non-stop tirade of swearwords, oaths, curses of a complex nature and colourful observations about the intricate circumstances leading up to

Jim's conception and birth, including many curious references to the female form and the sexual act.

John Smith left the field, regained his composure and considered the matter closed. And so it was; that is, until the following week.

Unfortunately for John Smith, amongst the few spectators near where the incident took place were the Reverend Green, the local representative of the Society for the Propagation of Religion, and his daughter, the lovely Miss Patience Green.

A few days after the match, John Smith was surprised to receive a letter from the Reverend Green, complaining about his outrageous conduct and informing him that he intended to apply for a summons against him under the Profane Oaths Act of 1745, and would be asking for a date for a hearing before the magistrates.

It was said that this Act had been promulgated in 1745 as a result of the unacceptable behaviour of Bonnie Prince Charlie, the Young Pretender, after he and his fellow Jacobite rebels had lost, decisively, the crucial home match at Culloden against the English, captained by the Duke of Cumberland. Apparently, as he left the field en route for France, His Would-be Majesty directed a string of oaths and curses in the Scottish vernacular at his team. The authorities felt that this sort of conduct brought rebelling into disrepute and introduced the 1745 Act in an effort to prevent any repetition.

John Smith asked the Prof to look into the provisions of the Act and was not unduly concerned when the Prof, in his usual long-winded way, reported, 'I have, at your request, read the provisions of the Act, and whilst the language in which it is written is rather more than somewhat old-fashioned, you will be relieved to learn that if guilty, the fine stated in the Act is a mere 12 pence, which in 1745 was, no doubt, a considerable sum, but today could be described as quite a trivial amount.'

John Smith was reassured, but his freedom from worry was short-lived because subsequently the Prof discovered that since 1745, there had been a ruling by a judge in a decided case that the fines applied not to oaths in general but to each individual oath. It became necessary therefore for the magistrates to know precisely how many oaths John Smith had uttered.

At the hearing both the Reverend Green and John Smith chose to represent themselves.

When the magistrates asked how he pleaded, John Smith replied, 'Not guilty,' and took the opportunity to assure the court that he was the mildest of men, kind to animals, fond of children, helped old people across the road, collected butterflies and enjoyed the ballet. He added that the dropped pass had resulted in his complete loss of self-control, offered his apologies and stated that he pleaded not guilty on the grounds of intolerable provocation.

The magistrates then asked the Reverend Green to address the court and outline the basis of his case, which he proceeded to do clearly and succinctly.

John Smith, in his turn to address the court, acknowledged that the facts complained of by the Reverend Green were substantially correct, but he disputed the number of oaths that the Reverend Green claimed that he had uttered. One hundred and fifty was a gross exaggeration. He would admit to only 'several oaths'.

Neither the Reverend Green nor John Smith chose to exercise their right to cross-examine the other.

The chairman of the magistrates stated that, in view of the fact that the amount of the fine would be calculated on the number of oaths uttered by John Smith, it was necessary to establish precisely what that number was. As he understood, the lovely Miss Patience Green, daughter of the Reverend Green, was the only witness and had been within earshot when the incident occurred; he therefore suggested that the Reverend Green call her as a witness, in order to repeat as many of the assorted oaths as she could remember.

The Reverend Green immediately sprang to his feet to point out to the court that his daughter had had a genteel upbringing, was of a delicate disposition and could not possibly sully her pretty lips, not to mention her chaste reputation, with such crude and uncouth words.

The chairman, whilst expressing his sympathy, asserted that Miss Green was not obliged to give evidence and excused her from so doing. The demure Miss Green gave the magistrates a nervous, sweet smile to show her appreciation of being relieved of such a distasteful duty.

The chairman then announced that he would adjourn the court to give time for the Reverend Green and John Smith to compromise on the number of oaths uttered.

The magistrates, on their return, were told that a compromise number of 60 had been agreed upon. This would equate to a possible fine of 60 times 12 pence, making three pounds in old money, no doubt a sizable sum in 1745.

Exercising his right to address the court, John Smith claimed that he was well-known as a local sportsman and respected for his magnanimity in victory and his calm acceptance of defeat; in fact, his reputation was envied by all sportsmen who knew him. His behaviour was, therefore, completely out of character. He ended by asking the magistrates to take these facts into account during their deliberations.

The Reverend Green in his address to the court pointed out that what Mr Smith said was all very well but, unless steps were taken now to stamp out this sort of conduct, it could happen that spectators would, in the future, begin to feel free to vocally criticise players during a match, possibly using ill-chosen words, and where would we be then?

The magistrates then withdrew to consider their verdict.

Most of the foregoing proceedings proved to have been superfluous, because on their return the chairman stated that he and his fellow magistrates had considered the matter in great detail. As a rugby player himself, he had experienced similar provocation during a match and could well sympathise with Mr Smith. He pointed out that the Act had been promulgated in 1745, a time when the game of rugby had been a leisure pursuit of but a few, and those drafting the statute were unlikely to have been familiar with the game or to have been aware of the emotions that could be aroused. In addition, the Act was of great antiquity and seldom used. For those reasons, the magistrates were unanimous in their view that the Profane Oaths Act 1745 did not apply in this particular case. John Smith, therefore, could leave the court without a stain on his character.

After the case, the demure Miss Patience Green was heard to say, 'The whole bloody case was a fucking stitch-up; those bastards on the bench were a loadofshits.'

So much for the lovely Miss Patience Green's genteel upbringing and delicate disposition.

MISS MASTERS

At one end of the ground was a terrace of Victorian houses, their gardens protected by a fence backed on to the area behind the goal posts. Rugby balls from conversions or penalties often landed in the gardens. Usually, the house-owners returned the balls; that was, with one exception: Miss Phyllis Masters.

At the beginning of each season, it was the custom of the rugby club to invite the residents of the terrace to a cocktail party held in the club premises. Miss Masters was invited, arrived and appeared to be thoroughly enjoying socialising until she witnessed the 3rd XV's performance of their well-known rendition of *Swing Low, Sweet Chariot* accompanied by their graphic and original actions. Clearly, she did not approve. Soon after, and well before the end of the party, she stormed out of the bar, vociferously claiming that someone had pinched her bottom.

Through a member of the rugby club who was wooing one of Miss Masters' maids, Mary West, it was learned that Miss Masters was of a religious disposition and, as a result of attending the cocktail party, considered the rugby club to be a den of iniquity and the members uncouth in the extreme and beyond redemption. More worrying was the fact that, as a protest, she was refusing to return any rugby balls landing in her garden. According to Mary West, no amount of pleading would persuade her to change her mind.

She steadfastly refused even to discuss the matter with a representative of the rugby club.

The following Saturday, from each of two conversion attempts, the ball landed in the garden of Miss Masters.

This was extremely worrying because the club's stock of balls was always kept to a minimum and those left were not really up to the required standard, most not being properly inflated. What would happen if the third ball went over the fence?

One did, whereupon Doubledick and Jim Lambert rushed to the fence and Doubledick instructed Jim to climb over. When the fence proved to be too high, Doubledick unceremoniously grabbed Jim and lobbed him over. This sudden act was immediately followed by the sound of breaking glass and Jim's anguished cry, 'You've dropped me in the middle of some cold frames.'

Doubledick shouted, 'Don't worry about the bloody cold frames; just get the fucking balls.'

Jim collected the three balls and threw them over the fence to Doubledick, who rushed back to the waiting players.

At this point, Jim was horrified to realise that, unaided, he couldn't climb over the fence, nor could he locate in the garden anything which would enable him to do so. He had no choice but to leave through the house.

He walked up the garden path and knocked on the back door, coming face to face with a startled and then irate Miss Masters. Jim said, as politely as he was able, 'Good afternoon, Miss Masters. Would you be so kind as to permit me to leave your premises by the front door?'

Miss Masters, speechless with fury, stepped aside and, tight-lipped, ushered Jim through her house, his muddy boots leaving bits of earth on the kitchen floor and smudges on the hall carpet as he hurried through to the front door.

Jim, in full rugby kit, still had to walk 50 yards down a busy road before turning in to a short lane to the rugby pitch, where he was greeted by Doubledick. 'Where the bloody hell have you been? Don't you know we are playing one man short?'

The Miss Masters problem was on the agenda of the next committee meeting, but there was no agreement as to what, if any, action could be taken to ensure that future balls landing in Miss Masters' garden could be retrieved.

After the meeting, during drinks and informal discussion of the matter in the bar, Izzy Soloman was present. He listened intently, then said, 'Leave it to me. I'll sort the problem,' but refused to divulge what he proposed to do.

Izzy, although he had never played rugby, was a member and keen supporter of the rugby club. He was a plausible middle-aged widower with bright red hair who owned and tended a small-holding on which he grew a range of fruit and vegetables. Early each morning, he would load his costermongers' barrow with produce and push it to the nearby town market, returning in the late afternoon with, hopefully, an empty barrow and a pocketful of cash. He was popular, always cheerful, and he and his barrow were a familiar sight in the area. He enjoyed a reputation as a voracious 'ladies' man'. This, together with his ginger hair, resulted in a question mark as to the biological father of any child born in the area with red hair.

Izzy's tactics with Miss Masters were quite simple. Each day, at about 4.30 in the afternoon, on his return from the market, he would park his barrow outside the entrance of Miss Masters' terraced house. As this house faced on to a busy road between the shops and the bus station, numerous passers-by noticed the barrow. Because of Izzy's reputation the implication was obvious.

Within two days, Miss Masters deputed Mary West to remonstrate with Izzy about his parking outside her house. During the conversation, Izzy mentioned the problem with the rugby balls.

Thereafter, Miss Masters made a particular point of being expeditious in returning rugby balls that landed in her garden. It was said that on Saturday afternoons she stood in her garden prepared to catch and return rugby balls just as soon as she could.

Early the next season, Miss Masters received the customary invitation to the rugby club's beginning-of-the-season cocktail party. She declined with regret... or so she said.

JESSIE AND DOUBLEDICK

One November, Doubledick, baptismal name Richard Richards, the 3rd XV scrum-half, had the temerity to announce that he was shortly to be propelling his girlfriend, Jessie, up the aisle.

Jessie was the sister of the Prof, who resolutely guarded her from the attentions – not always honourable – of the rugby club members. Jessie was a happy-go-lucky character, slightly plump but always quick to point out that, 'I am not fat; I am voluptuous, if anybody wants to know.' She possessed flashing dark brown eyes with matching hair hanging down each side of her fresh, round, dimpled face, which always seemed to conceal a smile or a giggle waiting to break through. Her lips hinted at a passionate nature, and invariably she dressed very simply in an embroidered wench-like blouse and flowing skirt which emphasised her curvaceous appearance; very attractive to the opposite sex. Wives and girlfriends of members, particularly of the 3rd XV, kept a watchful eye on their men when Jessie was in the vicinity.

For some time it had been obvious to members of the rugby club that the relationship between Jessie and Doubledick was becoming increasingly close. As Billyoddsocks observed, until they were actually married, there was still hope – slender though it might be – of capturing Jessie's affections; Doubledick might fall under the proverbial tram. Billyoddsocks was somewhat irritated when Eggie pointed out that the nearest tram was 50 miles away in London.

To the 3rd XV this was good news because for the last six months or so Jessie, in the capacity of Doubledick's girlfriend, had been 'doing the teas'. It was generally agreed that Jessie was a dab hand at sandwich-making and brewed a first-class cup of tea.

However, consternation was caused when Doubledick announced that the ceremony would take place in two weeks on Saturday at three o' clock. There was an immediate outburst of questions from the 3rd XV. Why a Saturday and why at three o' clock? What sort of team-man are you? Where does your loyalty lie? Why can't you arrange to marry Jessie in the summer, or at least be considerate enough to postpone the nuptials until April, when you could combine your honeymoon with the Easter Tour?

Doubledick explained that there were cogent reasons, which he was not prepared to discuss in detail, why the wedding needed to be as soon as possible. Doubledick did concede that he would approach his future in-laws, who would be footing the bill for the celebrations, to ask if they would agree to the ceremony being held instead at eleven o' clock. Theoretically this would enable the 3rd XV to be present in his hour of need, and also make it possible for the 3rd XV to honour its fixture on that Saturday. He continued that he was sure that the 3rd XV understood that he had no choice but to attend the reception, and therefore would be unavailable for selection. In any case, on his wedding day, it was not a rugby ball he should be putting in. Doubledick could be rather more than somewhat uncouth at times.

A few days later, Billyoddsocks and Eggie in the nearby town happened to encounter Doubledick.

Doubledick mentioned that he had just purchased the diamond ring with which he intended to plight his troth to

45

Jessie. The ring he produced for examination was rather on the small side, and it needed to be held at a particular angle in a strong north light to be seen at its best.

It was formally agreed that the 3rd XV, instead of several small presents, would give the happy couple a collective wedding present, the matter to be discussed at training the following Thursday.

Under 'Any Other Business', it was, after a protracted discussion, agreed that '*Each member shall contribute a like sum.*' But how much?

Billyoddsocks suggested, 'Two shillings?'

'What's wrong with three shillings?' I asked.

Eggie said, 'What's wrong with five shillings?'

'What's wrong with six shillings?' said the Prof.

And Billyoddsocks said, 'What was wrong with two shillings?'

So two shillings it was.

The financial commitment for the wedding present having been decided, the question arose, 'Is there anything Doubledick needs?'

The answer came speedily from Billyoddsocks. 'He certainly needs some new jock-straps. Did you see the tatty one he was wearing last week?'

Whilst heads were nodding in agreement, the Prof stepped in. 'I feel bound to state that as the event we propose to commemorate with a gift is a marriage between two persons of differing sex, that is, a man and a woman, it is incumbent on us that the aforementioned gift must be such as to be acceptable to and enjoyed by both participants. I suspect that most of you are aware that the current standard design of the female form does not include anything to put in a jock-strap...'

Billyoddsocks had the nerve to interrupt the Prof, saying, 'Well, what about a jock-strap for Doubledick and a bra for Jessie? She has plenty to put in a bra.'

Several of those present smiled lasciviously, as they nodded in agreement.

The Prof, undeterred, continued, 'The difficulty would then arise as to which size?'

Immediately, all present stretched out their arms in front of themselves with each hand in the form of a cup.

The Prof started again. 'I greatly appreciate your collective desire to be of help, but I feel that I should point out that it is not obvious which of your demonstrations is likely to be the most accurate. Even if this fact could be ascertained, it would be difficult for the person designated to make the proposed purchase to translate this vital information to the sales lady behind the lingerie counter. I understand that in shops selling this kind of apparel the measurement is required to be to the nearest inch, but from your demonstrations, in Jessie's case, it appears that the nearest foot would be acceptable.'

Despite several offers to measure Jessie's bust, it was obvious that it would be difficult to arrange to do this without alerting Jessie to the reason the information was required.

Because no further suggestions were put forward, it was agreed that there was no solution to the problem and the matter was dropped, much to the disappointment of those present. Everyone had enjoyed discussing Jessie's measurements, busts being a subject on which all felt that they could make an informed contribution, some better than others. No doubt, reliving nostalgic memories of what might have been.

Ultimately, Eggie purchased a porcelain pepper and salt set: two rabbits, embracing.

Early on the Great Day, there was a collective sigh of relief when it was learned that, owing to a heavy frost the previous night, the ground had become unplayable, and therefore that day's match was cancelled.

With the bells of St George's pealing, Jessie arrived, resplendent in a white silk bridal gown. She entered the church traditionally, ten minutes late, on the arm of her father, and accompanied by four bridesmaids.

It was only then that the hearts were finally broken and hopes dashed of several members of the rugby club. Undaunted, these members were soon sizing up the bridesmaids for a suitable replacement for Jessie in their fantasies.

The members of the 3rd XV in their dapper gents' suiting, clean (presumably) shirts and ties, armed with packets of confetti and rice, were present in strength in the church. There was disappointment amongst them at the absence of *Swing Low, Sweet Chariot* from the list of hymns.

The reception was held in the village hall, at one end of which were two large tables displaying wedding presents. Just before the celebrations began, Doubledick came up to me and asked if I would be so kind as to keep an eye on the presents because, he said, 'There will be a few light-fingered people here today.'

I asked, 'Why did you invite them, then?'

He explained, 'We had to. They are family.'

Because I took my responsibilities of guarding the wedding presents seriously, I remained close by the tables, which were situated a short distance from the hard core of the guests. In a typical demonstration of fraternal concern, first one 3rd XV member, then another, brought me a drink to sustain me during my vigil.

After a short while, I realised that these kind and thoughtful acts had gradually impaired my safeguarding abilities. Anyone could have stolen the table, let alone a present, for all I would have noticed. I gave up and joined the rest of the guests. Fortunately for my reputation, no presents were reported missing.

The usual speeches were made, one by the vicar, who solemnly stated, 'This marriage of Jessie and Richard marks the end of a friendship begun in schooldays,' and was puzzled by the laughter this provoked.

The Prof, with his reputation for being long-winded, was persuaded not to make a speech because the hall was booked for a whist drive beginning in six hours' time.

Amid much hilarity, the newly-weds were sent on their way, an assortment of pots and pans attached to the bumper of their car with dubious matrimonial advice written in whitewash on the roof.

The wedding of Doubledick and Jessie was considered by the members of the rugby club to be a most enjoyable occasion. The 3rd XV behaved very well; that is, if you ignore the fact that a member (and I wish to remain anonymous) accidently knocked over the three-tiered wedding cake.

The bride and groom returned from their honeymoon on the following Friday evening so that on the Saturday Doubledick could play for the 3rd XV and Jessie could do the teas. It was established practice that any young lady marrying a member of the 3rd XV in effect married the club.

Jessie continued masterminding the teas for a total of 37 years, including four after the death of Doubledick. This came about because, on the envelope containing Doubledick's will, he had written, '*It is my dying wish that my legal wife, Jessie, carries on doing the 3rd XV teas.*'

The Prof couldn't resist the opportunity to point out, at length, 'Whilst we all greatly appreciate the kind and thoughtful action of our late team-mate and friend... I think that all of you are aware that I do not claim to have any professional legal training or experience of the law. However, I am of the opinion that, as the signature of our lately departed dear friend was not witnessed, Jessie is under no binding obligation to honour Doubledick's dying wish...'

As the Prof paused to take a breath before continuing, Billyoddsocks broke in to report that Jessie had stated she would insist on honouring Doubledick's dying wish.

The Prof calculated that Jessie had produced over the years more than 40 000 teas. The Prof was more than somewhat smart when it came to sums.

At Jessie's funeral, a deputation of members of the 3rd XV, past and present, placed an old, battered aluminium teapot, filled with lilies, on the top of her coffin. This simple act was considered by all concerned to be an appropriate and most touching gesture.

Over tea at the wake after Jessie's funeral, Eggie suggested, 'Jessie should have been immortalised.'

This led to a lively discussion.

Beebie, somewhat shocked, said, 'I thought that was what they do to Egyptian mummies.'

The Prof said, 'No, that's embalming.'

Beebie asked, 'Is that what Jessie died of, then?'

The Prof explained, 'A person is immortalised if he, or she, commits an act or series of acts, all of which are considered to be so remarkable to all concerned that he, or she, should never be forgotten'

Billyoddsocks said, 'Like score a try for the 3rd XV. Ha, ha.'

'Well, not really...' said the Prof.

'What about two tries, three tries?' said Eggie.

'If anyone did that they would get a bloody statue.'

Feeling that he had lost control of the conversation, the Prof stated, pompously, 'Yes, but to be immortalised for scoring three tries for the 3rd XV those aforesaid three tries would have to be scored on the same day in the same match.'

The Prof sat back, confident that he had concluded the matter. Instead his pronouncement stimulated a further confused discussion, everyone talking at once about how three tries could/could not be scored in the same/different matches on the same/different days. A long wait was anticipated before any member of the 3rd XV scored three tries in a season, let alone in one match.

Jessie and Doubledick were responsible for producing a son and grandsons, all of whom in later years played in the 5th XV, the spiritual successor to the 3rd XV.

BEEBIE AND THE CHURCH CLOCK

The happenings concerning Beebie Brown and the church clock became part of the folklore of the rugby club.

Charles Brown had been brought up by stern parents, his father being a pillar of the local branch of the Temperance Society. For that reason, pubs and rugby club bars were strictly out-of-bounds for young Charles. To quench his thirst of an evening, Charles was regularly seen running from his home to the local off-licence to purchase a bottle of beer. He would, still running and with the bottle concealed about his person, return home. When the opportunity arose, he would sneak in to the garden shed and there enjoy his beer He became generally known as 'Beer Bottle Brown' or 'Beebie Brown' for short.

Beebie was below average in stature, rotund with a cherubic face surmounted by thinning hair, a few strands of which were combed from one side of his head to the other in an unsuccessful attempt to conceal his imminent total baldness. A member of the rugby club for two seasons before the Great War, he had shown great promise as an aggressive and unflagging scrum-half. He was always cheerful and helpful but unwilling to fill any offices of the rugby club.

Beebie had badgered the recruiting authorities until they had accepted him, at an early age, into the army, and had served in the latter part of Great War, although well behind the front line he had been wounded by a random shell *Somme*-where in France. Thereafter, he walked with a slight limp. Demobbed, he rejoined the rugby club hoping to resume playing, but the 3rd XV were, on the advice of the club committee, required to turn down his request to be considered for selection because:

> *whilst great skill at rugby was not necessarily a required qualification to play for the 3rd XV, Rule 12(a) of the Constitution of the Club provided that all playing members must be sound in mind, wind and limb.*

The committee further stated that they interpreted this rule as embracing all three; a mere majority was not acceptable.

Beebie's disappointment was assuaged when he received a letter from the committee stating that in view of his distinguished and selfless service during the recent World War, they would be delighted to offer him the post of official linesman of the 1st XV.

Beebie replied: '*Whilst I understand the reason I cannot be considered for selection, I appreciate the great honour offered to me by the committee, but if it is all the same to the said committee, I would prefer to be the official linesman of the 3rd XV.*'

The committee, in their wisdom, acceded to Beebie's request.

Beebie placated his father by pointing out that he was over 21 years of age, had suffered wounds defending his country, and he was fucking well going to enjoy his beer in pubs, rugby clubs, houses of ill repute and anywhere else that happened to be within reach when he was thirsty, including at times when he didn't feel thirsty.

Beebie took his appointment very seriously, turning up every Saturday, both home and away, fully kitted for play, and rarely missing a match. After a long kick into touch, he sometimes, because of his limp, arrived a minute or two late, in which case a helpful spectator or one of the players would kindly show him where the ball had gone out and which team's throw-in it was.

On one occasion at a home match against local rivals, the 3rd XV had built up their customary first-half lead but now were only four points ahead, with the final whistle due in a few minutes. The visitors scored a try. The 3rd XV were greatly relieved when the conversion was missed.

Could the tiring 3rd XV, now only one point in the lead, hold out against the relentless attacks of the visitors for the few remaining minutes of play? Beebie, emotionally involved as he was, realised that, more than likely, the 3rd XV could not; time was not on the side of the 3rd XV and drastic action needed to be taken, urgently.

Suddenly he thrust his flag into the hands of a startled middle-aged lady watching the match, whispering, 'Take the line,' and ran off in the direction of the church. This he entered and, forgetting his limp, he ran up the spiral steps to the upper reaches of the tower where the internal mechanism of the church clock was situated. Traditionally referees timed the matches by this ancient timepiece.

His plan was to ease forward the minute hand of the clock a few minutes in order to save the 3rd XV from a defeat which appeared to be a strong possibility.

Rather than disturb the clock just before it was due to chime at four o'clock, Beebie decided to wait until it had done so. Whilst waiting for the clock to reach four, he sat on part of the clock's rambling wooden structure. When he made to stand up, he discovered that, to his horror, part of his rugby shorts had become entangled with the cogwheels of the mechanism of the clock. The cogs continued to turn remorselessly. What if it's an eight-day clock? he thought...

Beebie, having finally struggled free from his shorts, realised that he had no choice but to abandon them, ensnared in the clock's mechanism, until the cogwheel had completed a full circle.

Slowly, he carefully eased the minute-hand of the clock ahead by five minutes while he waited for the release of his shorts, which, it now appeared, would take at least half an hour.

What now? Appearing through the door of the pavilion wearing only rugby boots, jock-strap, socks and a shirt might, even amongst the 3rd XV members, cause a certain amount of comment and ribald remarks. He couldn't collect a pair of shorts from his home in the middle of the village, because a trouserless man would be arrested on sight.

Beebie realised that he would have to stay near the clock until the offending cog had turned full circle, releasing his shorts, when he could return to the pavilion as if nothing had happened. He couldn't leave the clock and return when his shorts were about to be released, because each time the cog met the tooth of the next cog, to avoid the risk of the clock stopping, it was necessary to carefully guide the shorts on in the direction of the approaching tooth. Beebie was compelled to remain trouserless and trapped in the church tower for some time yet.

Meanwhile, back on the pitch, the 3rd XV had survived to record a narrow victory. Beebie's strange conduct had not gone unnoticed. Where was he?

When the middle-aged lady had handed in the linesman's flag and was asked, 'Where's the linesman?' she stated, rather forcefully, that she didn't know and couldn't care less.

Eggie said he had seen Beebie near the church, which he was known to frequent only for weddings and funerals, and not many of the latter at that.

Billyoddsocks, Doubledick and the Prof volunteered to visit the church, just in case. Once inside they shouted, 'Is there anyone here?'

To their surprise a faint voice replied, 'Up here.' The reply was unmistakably in Beebie's voice.

'Where's up here?'

Through that small door in the corner.'

'Where's the light switch?'

'There isn't one.'

'I can't hear you, speak up.'

'I can't! Someone might hear me.'

The three rescuers struggled up the spiral stairs in almost pitch darkness amongst shushes and guffaws, plus the odd expletive when heads were bumped on the low stone ceiling.

There was Beebie, sitting without his shorts on the framework surrounding the clock mechanism, well away from the cogs. As the Prof observed some time later, 'Not a pretty sight.'

It was generally agreed that it would be at least another 20 minutes, possibly longer, before Beebie's shorts could be released and recovered from the cogwheels. The Prof offered to stay with Beebie, who claimed that he was 'dying of thirst', whilst Billyoddsocks and Doubledick returned, clandestinely, to the bar to obtain four pints of beer, one for each of them.

It was important that the purchase of the beers should be done unobtrusively so that the cause of Beebie's predicament should not leak out whilst members of the afternoon's opponents' team were still drinking at the bar. Billyoddsocks and Doubledick purchased and smuggled two pints of beer each through a throng of animated rugby players and slipped out of the bar. Billyoddsocks' suggestion of taking a short cut across the ground was not a good idea because he forgot that the cricket square was surrounded by low chains for the winter, which, the chains not being noticeable in the twilight, he stumbled over, spilling some of the precious beer down his trousers.

Beebie drank the life-saving beer, then, finally united with his slightly tattered rugby shorts, he and his stalwart rescuers were free to leave. As Beebie was still wearing his linesman's kit, Billyoddsocks and Doubledick offered to sneak into the changing room, casually purloin his clothes and give them to Beebie, who would then avoid the bar area by slipping into the groundsman's storage shed. There, unnoticed, he would change into his casual clothes and then mingle with the crowd in the bar as if he had been there all the time.

Inside the shed, Beebie was just about to divest himself of his rugby kit when he noticed through the window of the shed well-known ladies' man Tommy Bates coming out of the bar, affectionately accompanied by Kitty Johnson, who had a reputation for being generous in bestowing her feminine favours on the male sex. Both took several deep breaths. Beebie wasn't surprised because on Saturday evenings the bar was overcrowded and became very stuffy.

Beebie then realised that they were walking in the direction of the groundsman's shed. They arrived at the door and began fumbling with the lock for a while before getting the door open and entering the shed. Beebie was obliged to hurriedly conceal himself amongst the rollers, sight screens, tennis nets, garden equipment and all kinds of other summer clutter and remain motionless.

After some muttering, giggles, *oh*s and *ah*s, the two intruders began taking deeper and deeper breaths. Beebie was puzzled because, in his opinion, the air in the shed was not particularly fresh; probably, the door hadn't been opened since the end of the cricket season. Then quite suddenly they stopped taking deep breaths and, after more muttering, left the shed.

Beebie's great relief at their departure was short-lived, because to reassure himself he glanced through the shed window and saw Tommy and Kitty pause just short of the bar. Tommy turned and began determinedly to walk back in the direction of the shed. With no time to conceal himself again, Beebie froze; Tommy burst in through the door to be confronted by Beebie in his rugby kit without his shorts.

Tommy said, 'What the fucking hell are you doing here?'

Beebie lamely answered, 'It is a long story.'

Tommy: 'I should think it bloody well is. How long have you been here?'

Beebie: 'About a quarter of an hour, I think.'

Tommy realised the significance of Beebie's answer and said, menacingly, 'Well, just keep your fucking mouth shut.' After a short pause to allow Beebie to receive and understand the instruction, Tommy said, 'My friend thinks that she dropped her wrist-watch somewhere here.' Despite insufficient twilight coming through the shed window, he fell to his knees and began feeling with his hands all over the dirty floor, but couldn't locate the missing wrist-watch.

Beebie was only just able to contain his laughter at the bizarre and aberrant scene in the twilight.

Tommy stood up to leave and said, 'I can't find the fucking watch.'

Neither Beebie nor Tommy could think of any parting pleasantries which would be appropriate in the circumstances. Tommy stormed out of the shed, slamming the door.

Beebie, having at last changed into his clothes, was about to leave the shed when he noticed an old broom in the corner. Quick-thinking, he used it to sweep the floor, found the wrist-watch and put it in his pocket, not knowing what he intended to do with it.

Beebie, now properly attired, unobtrusively entered the bar, studiously avoiding Tommy. On the one occasion when they did meet, Tommy quietly hissed, 'Remember: keep your fucking mouth shut.'

Beebie: 'It depends.'

Tommy: 'Depends on what?'

Beebie replied, 'You'll see,' and slipped away into the crowd at the bar, leaving a worried Tommy.

Beebie and Tommy next met at a formal meeting between representatives of the club and Tommy concerning the second pitch adjacent to the main pitch. The continued use of this pitch was vital to the rugby club; without it, when there were two home matches, the 3rd XV would have to play on the pitch of the local school situated on the other side of the town. The pitch had been rented at a nominal rent from Charles Pratt, a life-long member and supporter of the rugby club, who had recently died. Tommy Bates had made an offer to the executors of the estate of Charles Pratt to purchase the pitch, intending to sell it, at an inflated price, to the rugby club.

At the meeting Beebie contrived to sit next to Tommy, who was adamant that he would not withdraw his offer.

During a recess at the meeting, Beebie leaned over towards Tommy, saying, 'My watch seems to have stopped working. Can you tell me the time?'

Tommy consulted his own watch, told Beebie the correct time and watched Beebie roll up the sleeve of his jacket and ostentatiously move the hands on the watch. Tommy immediately realised that Beebie was wearing Kitty's watch. Their eyes met until Beebie said, 'Do you really want to make money out of the club's second pitch?

Tommy was silent. The meeting continued for a few minutes. Three days later, Tommy withdrew his offer and Charles Pratt's widow agreed a new lease with the rugby club at a nominal rent, saying, as she signed the documents, 'That's what Charles would have wanted.'

Beebie dropped the wrist-watch through Kitty's letter box; anonymously, of course.

The whole episode had its plus side because the fact that the church clock was several minutes fast was soon noticed. Experts called in reported that there was no sign of any maintenance for the last 100 years, possibly more, and that repairs were urgently required because one of the wooden supports of a bell was dangerously infected with woodworm and on the verge of collapsing.

Just after the incident it was learned that the curate, when passing the church that Saturday afternoon, had noticed curious shadows on the brightly lit clock face, not knowing it was caused by Beebie moving around behind. The curate was convinced it was a vision.

Seeing a lady walking around the side of the church, he shouted to her, 'Quick! Quick! Come and look at the church clock!'

He was greatly disappointed when the vision was not repeated, and said to the puzzled lady, 'What a pity it didn't happen again. That sort of thing is awfully good for business.'

ATTEMPTED GRAND LARCENY

For some reason I cannot now remember, one of the regular opponents of the 3rd XV was forced on the Friday morning to cancel the match for the following day.

The 3rd XV were greatly disappointed. After all that training and tactical planning, a match on Saturday was much needed.

During the Friday, the match secretary, through someone who knew someone else, found a team willing to play on the Saturday.

On that Friday evening, most of the 3rd XV, rejoicing that a last-minute substitute team had been found, arrived at the rugby club bar to learn that the match secretary had deputed Johnny Watkins to provide information about Saturday's opponents. Gathered around the bar, clutching their pints of beer, the 3rd XV waited expectantly for Johnny to speak.

He began by stating that the team were the Chilton Bandits, who, because they were based about 40 miles away, would be travelling by charabanc and arrive at two o' clock for a 2.30 kick-off. They needed to depart at 6.30 in order to attend a social occasion back at base. He added that he been asked by the match secretary to contact the Chilton Bandits to confirm the timings and to sort out any problems.

Johnny's explanation brought forth a confusion of questions: 'Where's Chilton?' 'Never heard of it, or them!'

'Who do they play against?' 'How good are they?' 'How many teams do they run?'

The chorus of questions overwhelmed Johnny, but he was given time to collect his thoughts when one member of the 3rd XV said, 'I seem to remember that there is a girls' secondary school in Chilton!'

The lascivious thoughts of scrummaging with a group of nubile girls interrupted the flow of questions. The pause enabled the Prof to step in to call for silence. 'I am sorry to disappoint you all. There are no records of girls playing rugby, but perhaps, who knows, in the future?'

Turning to Johnny, he continued, 'I understand that you are to contact a representative of the Chilton Bandits to arrange times and any other matters about which the 3rd XV requires reassurance. Presumably, you will do this by telephone and are therefore in possession of the relevant number. May I suggest that, whilst we are all present, you telephone that number and obtain answers to our many questions?'

The Prof's suggestion was received with exclamations of approval. He leaned over the bar and handed the telephone to Johnny who felt in his pocket for a piece of paper which he consulted and then dialled the number. The telephone answered, Johnny stated his name and the subject of his call, then fell silent, listening intently.

The 3rd XV audience soon became restless and began urging Johnny to 'get on with it', and most of those present repeated, all talking at once, the many questions for which the members of the 3rd XV required answers.

Johnny stuttered down the telephone, 'J-j-j-just a minute.' He cupped his hand over the mouthpiece and addressed the waiting 3rd XV. 'He says that he much appreciates the fact that we are prepared to invite them to play, and that his team are all looking forward to the match and he has hopes that it will be the first of many fixtures. He said that he assumed our fixtures list was full for this season but perhaps a return match could be staged early next year. They will arrive in time for a 2.30 kick-off...'

Johnny was interrupted again by loudly shouted instructions: 'We know all that crap. Ask him who they play against, and how many teams; that's what we want to know!'

Johnny, flustered, put the telephone back to his ear and did as instructed. Then, falling silent again, he just listened. A few minutes more provoked assorted shouts urging him again to 'get on with it'.

Into the telephone, Johnny again said, 'J-j-j-just a minute,' and he again cupped a hand over the mouthpiece. 'He says that they play against local teams but don't have a headquarters. They play on the pitch of a nearby school but are negotiating with a local farmer for the use of one of his fields, which will take at least a year. He says that the rugby club was started only a short time ago and they do not yet have the usual fixture list. They also have a problem of members coming and going; some of the players have been members for only a short time and are still learning the finer points of playing rugby. He says that our match secretary said that this did not matter because the standard of play of our 3rd XV is not very high...'

This information provoked an emotional outburst from the 3rd XV. Some members started making some very uncouth remarks about the match secretary and his conduct, and some threatened to remove certain parts of his body.

Johnny, now agitated, shouted into the telephone, 'See you tomorrow at two o'clock!' He slammed it down and quickly left the bar in a flurry, relieved that his ordeal was over.

Digesting the little information they had received about their opponents, the 3rd XV could not help but feel uneasy. There did not appear to be sufficient time before the match to fraternise with the Chilton team, a tradition observed by all clubs on the 3rd XV fixture list.

Their enthusiasm for the match was not enhanced when disturbing rumours began circulating that the match secretary had inadvertently booked a team from a temperance society.

The 3rd XV couldn't make up their minds whether to enjoy their usual beers to inflame themselves to stirring deeds, or to take the match against the unknown Chilton team seriously and merely sip an odd beer or two. With the Chilton team having to depart at 6.30, there would be insufficient time to assess whether or not the Chilton Bandits should be appear on next year's fixture card.

Punctually at two o' clock, the charabanc arrived and out jumped a very mixed group, mostly in their late twenties accompanied by two middle-aged gentlemen, all clutching identical kitbags. They proceeded determinedly to the entrance to the club, entered, solemnly shook hands with a few bewildered members standing at the bar, asked for directions and disappeared into the visitors' changing room. The two gentlemen introduced themselves; the stocky, fat one explained that he drove the charabanc and the tall one wearing glasses stated that he was the referee whom Chilton had agreed to provide.

The 3rd XV did not like what they saw.

At 2.30 precisely, the Chilton team were drawn up on the pitch ready to kick off, the referee waiting to blow his whistle. Most of the 3rd XV were on the pitch with the exception of the captain, who was still searching for the match ball.

Billyoddsocks kicked off. The ball was caught cleanly by a Chilton player, who was immediately surrounded by his team-mates; they formed themselves into a battering ram which charged towards the 3rd XV line. When this was finally brought to a halt, the Chilton forwards quickly 'heeled' the ball and created another battering ram. The tactic was repeated until the final recipient was close enough to put his head down and make a resolute dash for the 3rd XV try-line. Because several of the backs of the Chilton Bandits became part of the battering ram, the 3rd XV could score only when they won the ball and fed their backs quickly, untroubled by the depleted and weakened Chilton defence.

During the half-time break, with the score 32 to 14 in Chilton's favour, Billyoddsocks said to Doubledick, 'This is not rugby. I'm sure that what they are doing is against the rules. This is not the sort of game we are used to playing. Some of their forwards must be offside.'

Doubledick replied, 'There is nothing we can do about it. We accepted their offer to bring a referee.'

The pattern of the second half was the same, Chilton winning the match 54 to 22. The 3rd XV had no answer to Chilton's tactics, becoming too exhausted, both physically and mentally, to care. Walking back to the clubhouse, Billyoddsocks said to Doubledick, 'I don't mind losing,' (actually, he did), 'but they had no sense of humour.'

After the players had changed and enjoyed one of Jessie's magnificent teas both teams adjourned to the bar, where the 3rd XV noticed that their visitors appeared to be surprisingly thirsty and were being discouraged by the two middle-aged men from drinking too much.

The 3rd XV did their best to entertain their visitors, but the latter didn't appear to be interested in fraternising with their hosts.

Just before six o'clock some of the visitors had begun drifting outside, presumably making for the charabanc, when bursting in through the entrance to the bar came Millie Wells, ardent 3rd XV supporter. She was excited and appeared quite dishevelled, waving her arms and shouting hysterically, 'Quick, quick! They are trying to steal our corner flag! Quick!'

A group of about ten lady supporters of the 3rd XV had just got off the local bus from town and, as they walked past the pitch, noticed four or five men trying to remove one of the corner flags. Without a thought, they had rushed to do battle to save the flag, whilst Millie had scurried to the bar to obtain reinforcements. Having delivered the call to arms, she returned just as speedily to the fray.

The 3rd XV members were slightly irritated by this disturbance of their post-match beer-drinking session, but, aware that their honour as gentlemen was at stake and goaded by Jessie, they hurriedly followed her to the vicinity of the threatened corner flag, to find it still *in situ* and the culprits getting the worst of the struggle with the girls.

With the arrival of Jessie and the gallant members of the 3rd XV, the men realised that they were out-numbered and doomed. The two middle-aged men appeared and proceeded to address them with a few words which could only be described as colourful and crystal clear as they ordered them to get into the charabanc. They meekly did so.

The triumphant girls, muddied and some with torn clothing, recovering in the bar, proudly exhibited their scratches and bruises. One warrior refused to display her cheek (lower left) on which she claimed to have incurred a large bruise. The 3rd XV considered her refusal to be most unsporting.

The bravery of the girls became part of the 3rd XV folklore.

With all the visitors safely in the charabanc, parting sentiments were being exchanged. One of the middle-aged men offered the advice, 'You ought to select two or three of those girls; they would certainly liven up your scrum!'

Billyoddsocks smiled and said 'I hope that you get back in time for the party.'

The man retorted, 'There's no bloody party, mate; this lot are trusties and we've got to get them back in their cells and locked up safely for the night by nine sharp. Sorry about the corner flag; old habits die hard.'

Billyoddsocks just stared wide-eyed at the man.

At the committee meeting the following Monday, it was unanimously resolved not to seek a return match.

COLLY'S MISJUDGEMENT

A morose and solemn man was often seen sitting in the rugby club bar, contemplating his ruined career and pondering over what life might have been but for the office Christmas party. He was John William Flower, better known as 'Colly' Flower, who lived alone on the outskirts of the village in a small cottage purchased with his commuted pension.

A member of the ruby club for many years, Colly was small in stature, lantern-jawed with a pointed nose supporting spectacles with thick black rims, which gave him a studious appearance confirmed by his lack of a sense of humour.

He always wore a dark suit, white shirt, stiff collar and a plain tie. Out of the breast pocket of his jacket peeped the tip of a white handkerchief. During conversation he had an irritating habit of fiddling with one of his cuffs.

His overall appearance was businesslike and efficient; his colleagues assumed that his accounts were in perfect order: no erasures or crossings out, and definitely no coffee stains.

The office Christmas party is a traditional function loosely perpetrated in the name of St Nicholas, and is an occupational hazard for the uninitiated for which no university studies, professional training or correspondence courses can provide adequate preparation.

Put at the same party the chairman and the managing director who suspects that he has a passion for the recently arrived secretary, who is coveted by the production director, who has a thing going with the managing director's wife, and you have a perfect recipe for a lively, stimulating and entertaining evening in front of plenty of enthusiastic, although somewhat imprecise, witnesses. Office discipline, so resolutely maintained throughout the year, is completely disrupted when, for a few hours, decorum and convention are abandoned and accumulated repressions are no longer subjugated but are released by those two hazards, alcohol and sex.

This is the story of Colly Flower, head of accounts, who, after many uneventful years poring over his ledgers and getting his sums right, finally came to the conclusion that life was passing him by and that his remarkable talent, as exemplified by his uncanny ability to place the debits and credits in the correct columns, would be better utilised in making far-reaching decisions at board level. He therefore resolved that he must do something dramatic to draw the attention of the chairman, Sir Richard Padmore, and the managing director to himself. What better than organising the company's first office Christmas party?

As is invariably the custom, such a party is preceded by a few alcoholic 'looseners' in the various departments, and Colly, anxious to conform to tradition, dispensed a selection of potent drinks in the accounts department. After a few tots, the usually meek and mild-mannered Colly, wearing his best suit and patterned shirt with matching tie, in a glow of alcohol-induced self-confidence, set off for the canteen. On entry, he encountered the Savile Row tailored back of the sales director, which, with relish, he slapped, and in a high-pitched voice he shouted above the throng, 'Merry Christmas, you stupid clot.'

Although the sales director smiled it was obvious he was not amused.

Unperturbed, Colly lurched on, confronting the personnel director with, 'Roses are red, violets are blue, this firm stinks and so do you.'

Neither was the personnel director amused.

Pausing only to grab something to eat, and to drink a tumbler of fruit cup specially devised by the laboratory department, Colly pressed on towards where members of staff of all ages, shapes and sizes were gyrating around the floor in a style of dancing which could only have been inspired by St Vitus.

Spotting the wife of the chairman unattended, Col, ever the opportunist, gallantly asked her to dance, forgetting, unfortunately, that he had a partly-eaten chocolate éclair in his right hand, which, coming into contact with her bare back, did little to endear him to her.

The high spot of Colly's attempt to gain much-desired recognition was the production of a short satirical sketch, written by himself and performed by several of the more daring members of the office staff.

The leading man was a rather pointed and exaggerated caricature of the managing director, portraying him as a money-grubbing egocentric who seduced widows, defrauded orphans and generally behaved in an anti-social and most obnoxious manner.

The leading lady was a buxom young girl with what appeared to be two melons in her sweater. All the staff were aware that the relationship between the managing director and his secretary was one of cosy informality. Colly only needed to look in the direction of the managing director to become aware that he certainly did not approve of these exaggerated references to what was a source of pride to the secretary and, no doubt, of gratification to the managing director himself. It was obvious that, between the occasional forced laughs the managing director made, he was busy mentally deciding on some disagreeable course of action against Colly, who would regret having presented his misplaced and ill-considered theatrical production.

To get his colleagues 'rolling in the aisles' before the final curtain, Colly adapted an old joke. 'My son was sent home from school today. When I enquired, "Why?", he replied that the teacher had asked each boy what his father did and he had told him, "My father manages a strip club in Soho."

'"Why did you say that?" I asked.

'"Well, you didn't expect me to admit that my father works for Padmore Reciprocating Pumps Limited, did you?"'

Venerable Chairman Padmore, although pretending to smile, was seen consulting his duplicated programme to ascertain the name of the author of this execrable extravaganza, who had the temerity to cast such unwarranted aspersions on a family name which, over many generations, had contributed so much to pumps in general and double reciprocating goggle pumps in particular.

Intoxicated, Colly surged off in the direction of the bar, where he downed another large glass of fruit cup now well spiked by the laboratory staff. Suddenly, he felt an irresistible desire to converse with Miss Jones, a new recruit to Colly's accounts department: a young lady well endowed by nature in the appropriate places.

Locating Miss Jones, Colly whisked her off in the direction of the stationery store, much to the annoyance of the production director, who had for some time been engrossed in addressing a series of remarks to Miss Jones's plunging neckline.

Later it was apparent to all those present that Colly had conducted a searching and thorough enquiry into Miss Jones's abilities and professional qualifications, because having emerged from the stationery store, and as Colly was steering her in the direction of the exit, Miss Jones was heard to announce in a penetrating voice that Mr Flower had been pleased to appoint her as his personal assistant.

The next working day, the office Christmas party was not over, certainly not for Colly. Members of staff, with smirks and nudges, engaged in juicy post-mortems of Colly's activities and exchanged whispered confidences, all exaggerated and embellished in the telling.

Having alienated all the directors, and, what was more serious, the managing director's wife, *and* lost the respect of the accounts department staff, Colly realised that he was forever now part of an unending office legend. His attempt to gain recognition had failed miserably. Early retirement was the only solution.

So, for several years, he was seen a dejected, hunched up figure, sitting in the rugby club bar. He was easily recognised because, whilst sipping his beer, he could be heard mumbling to himself, 'Office Christmas parties, office Christmas parties. Scrooge was right; Ebenezer Scrooge was bloody right.'

EDGAR'S FOLLY

The nickname of Robert Sharp was, not surprisingly, Razor, or Raz for short. His father had been a prominent member of both the rugby and the cricket clubs. After his playing days had ended, he had been an enthusiastic supporter of the clubs, hoping that his son would become a member of both and add sporting fame and lustre to the name of Sharp: a name which was somewhat short of these attributes.

Raz did as his father told him to and joined both clubs, but did not show any desire to become committed. When, after leaving school, he found a job paying a modest wage, he completely lost interest in field sports because matches were scheduled for Saturday afternoons, a time which interfered with his favourite sporting activity: gambling on the horses.

Just before Raz left school, his father gave him an expensive state-of-the-art cricket bat to encourage him to play cricket. Raz had no desire to do so. In order to augment his income sufficiently to finance his gambling, he enthusiastically took up someone's suggestion of raffling the cricket bat. Not surprisingly, the raffle was based on a horse race, the imminent Grand National. Assuming that there were 40 entries, 40 tickets were drawn from those sold, then from those 40 a second draw was made for each of the horses.

The first prize was of course the expensive state-of-the-art cricket bat, with cash prizes for the ticket-holders of those horses finishing in second and third place. In addition, to ensure that all the punters retained interest in the race until the end, there was a cash prize for 'the Last Horse Past the Post'.

Most of the raffle tickets were sold by Raz's school-mates on the basis of 'sell three get one free' and sales were brisk. Raz was much gratified, as the sale of raffle tickets had greatly exceeded his expectations.

After the race, several people arrived for the prize-giving. The three main prizes were presented. Raz then quoted, from the report of the race in the local newspaper, the name of the horse listed as being the Last Horse Past the Post.

Immediately there was a loud, determined protest. 'No, no, my horse, Speedy Boy, was the Last Horse Past the Post!'

Raz consulted the newspaper again and was able to reply, 'No, it says here in the newspaper that Speedy Boy fell at the fifth jump.'

'I know that, but Speedy Boy got up and finished the course and was the last horse past the post. When I bought my tickets nothing was said about the jockey having to be on the last horse past the post.'

Those present all joined in the discussion, splitting equally between whether or not a jockey was required to be seated on the Last Horse Past the Post.

The Prof, realising that his friend, Raz, was in an embarrassing situation, stepped in, saying, 'If you will forgive me for interrupting, in my opinion, it would require the wisdom of Solomon to make a decision acceptable to each of the two parties involved: namely, the holder of the ticket of the last horse and jockey past the post and the holder of the ticket of the last riderless horse past the post. I therefore suggest that Raz give a prize to each of the parties.

But I feel that I should point out that Raz's decision should not be considered as setting a precedent, and definitely must not be regarded as binding on the Jockey Club and/or any other official bodies connected with horse-racing.'

An intelligent and far-seeing man, the Prof.

Many listening to the Prof were somewhat nonplussed by the reference to Solomon because the only person of that name with whom they were acquainted was Izzy Soloman. He was certainly not noted for his wisdom, rather more for his womanising.

One of the dinner ladies at the local school won the first prize. Having two daughters, she had no use for a cricket bat (whether state-of-the-art or not) and was more than happy to accept Raz's cash offer of about a third of the retail price.

Raz had, from his first venture into horse-racing, made a cash surplus, and now he still owned the cricket bat.

Raz and another member of the 3rd XV, Jim Lambert of The Dropped Pass fame, were colleagues working for a firm of chartered accountants. It is common knowledge that people consider these firms and those working for them to be boring and silly old farts, but people are not aware that there is a plus side to working for a firm of chartered accountants. This firm employed, in the typing and filing department, ten pretty girls, including Judy (with the big boobs). Potentially, a significant compensation.

Raz, now in his early twenties, against determined competition of other suitors, had been resolutely pursuing the enchanting Judy to accompany him up the aisle. Raz's modest wage and lack of capital caused Judy to waver. A big win on the horses might just persuade her.

Raz's belief was that only by his single-mindedly accumulating knowledge of all the information and facts about individual horses would it become possible for him to pick winners. To this end he studied every book, newspaper, and magazine dealing with racehorses – and their current form – that he could locate.

Raz was not averse to consulting his sources during office hours. His desk was the usual two pillars of drawers with one drawer, waist high, in between. Books of reference, such as the News of the World racing yearbook, *Horses for Courses* and others, could be placed in the middle drawer, opened sufficiently to allow Raz to study the contents. Should any unwelcome visitor come into his office, Raz would just lean forward, ostensibly to dip his pen in the inkwell, his stomach automatically closing the drawer.

Because the profession of accountancy is demanding and requires constant concentration to get all those sums right, regular periods of rest are necessary. Raz and Jim would, at about eleven o' clock in the morning, adjourn for a coffee at Auntie's Café close by.

A regular customer of Auntie's was Charlie, whose professional occupation was that of steward at the leading local club for trainers and owners of horses.

As they began to get to know Charlie better, Raz said to Jim, 'Look, at the club, Charlie stands behind the bar serving drinks to all those trainers and owners, right? Obviously, he will overhear all kinds of loose talk and pick up lots of gossip and confidential information about horses and races. Let's ask him if he has any tips.'

After a few more visits to Auntie's, Raz plucked up courage to do just that, only to receive from Charlie a very curt and abrupt, 'I never give tips.'

Two or three weeks later, as the three of them were leaving Auntie's, Charlie said, out of the blue, 'You could do worse than put your money on Edgar's Folly in the fifth race on Saturday.'

Back in the office, Raz ridiculed Charlie's tip, claiming that Edgar's Folly was a gold-plated no-hoper, quoted at 25 to 1, and, in any case, he had already worked out which horse would win the fifth race.

An animated argument between Raz and Jim ensued, the latter's view being that, as Charlie had originally made it clear that he didn't give tips but had now volunteered a tip for no particular reason, it must be a very hot tip. The argument raged until as a compromise they agreed that they would each put one pound in the kitty and both would attend the races on Saturday. Depending on the odds, they would then make a decision after the fourth race about which horse to back in the fifth race: Raz's choice or Edgar's Folly.

On the Saturday, Raz and Jim went by bus to the races and took up a viewpoint from which they could watch most of each race. Small bets were placed on the first four races. Because the wins and losses were about equal, they still had the original total of two pounds in the kitty. What to bet on in the fifth race? The odds on Edgar's Folly had now lengthened to 40 to 1.

All the previous arguments were revisited, their judgement now slightly muddled by the intake of several beers between races. Five minutes before the fifth race, in a joint fit of bravado, they placed two pounds to win on Edgar's Folly at 40 to 1. 'Shit or bust,' Raz said in his sweet old-fashioned way.

Raz and Jim took up their chosen viewpoint close to the bookie who had taken their bet, and from where they could see the start and finish of the race. Raz had brought his binoculars, planning to give Jim a running commentary.

'They are off!' Raz shouted.

Edgar's Folly was submerged in a bunch of a dozen horses behind the leading horse, his jockey's colours, black and white checkerboard shirt and light blue cap, only barely distinguishable. For the next two or three hundred yards of the course, their view of the race was obscured by the corner of the grand stand.

When the horses emerged, Raz, looking through his binoculars, shouted, 'He's still in the bunch; no, he's moving up the bunch, yes, he's ahead! No, he isn't, he's amongst the leaders... no, he's falling back! No, he's not, he's about fifth!' Raz became hysterical. 'There's three of them, it's neck and neck...' Raz was now almost incoherent. 'It must be a dead heat!'

The horses, in a group, passed the winning post.

Jim yelled, 'Did he win?'

Raz shouted, 'I couldn't fucking see.'

Jim groaned.

A minute later the winner was announced. It was not Edgar's Folly.

Disconsolate, a pound each down the drain, Jim deliberately tore the betting slip into eight pieces, dropping them on the ground.

Suddenly, Raz shouted, 'Look, *the red flag has gone up*! That means that there is an official objection.'

An agonising wait followed before the announcement over the tannoy came that, following an objection, Edgar's Folly had been declared the winner.

Where was the betting slip? Theirs was not the only one that had been torn up and dropped on the ground.

Raz ordered Jim, 'Spit on your hands, hold them out and as I find the pieces I'll stick them on your hand. Grasp it with your other hand, and then we'll go to the bookie.'

Raz found seven of the pieces and with Jim, now, with hands containing the seven pieces clasped together, looking like a Hindu at prayer, they went to confront the bookie.

The bookie was a portly, solid gentleman, with a six-foot-tall thug standing beside him. Raz and Jim approached the bookie; Jim opened his hands, exposing the tattered seven-eighths of their betting slip. The bookie listened attentively whilst Raz explained what had happened.

The bookie thought for a moment and then said, 'Fuck off, I don't pay out on fucking jigsaws.'

To ensure that the bookie had not been misunderstood, the six-foot thug leaned forward, growling, 'Fuck off.'

Raz hesitated for a moment, then said, 'Wait there, Jim, I'll fetch the course marshal', a name he made up on the spur of the moment.

He had gone only a few yards when the bookie shouted, 'Laddie, come back. Wait a minute, laddie. Come back!'

On Raz's return, the bookie asked Jim to open his hands, contemplated the problem and, without a word, turned around to collect from a bulging leather bag a handful of notes from which he counted 82 pounds, the two-pound bet at 40 to 1 plus the stake.

Forty pounds in those days equated to more than six months' wages for Raz. He gave up gambling on the horses, using his windfall to upgrade his standard of courting Judy. They married a year later.

After his first visit to the races, in the taxi home (sod the bus), Jim observed, 'The bookmaking profession does seem to attract an uncouth class of practitioner with a remarkably limited vocabulary.'

Jim became addicted to playing the horses, and the local bookies gradually recovered what he had won on Edgar's Folly.

There's a moral there, somewhere.

TEAM SECRETARY

I became holder of the demanding office of team secretary only because at the club annual general meeting, when I returned from a quick visit to the loo, I discovered that in my absence I had been elected, unopposed and unanimously.

Ideally, at the Monday evening team selections meeting for three teams, there should be 45 players, all available to play in their preferred positions. The life of a team secretary is not like that. Instead, there would be any number but 45, often including six scrum-halves, rarely only the three required.

If players of the first or second teams became unavailable, the positions would be filled by players from the team below. The 3rd XV, being the bottom of the heap, was always the most disrupted. In those cases, I was further handicapped by the reluctance of the senior (by age) members of the 3rd XV to move up to the 2nd XV except in the direst of emergencies. Any ambition they had had to gain promotion had faded long ago. The reason they gave for not wanting to desert the 3rd XV was that only regular players were able to execute the intricate and complex moves developed over the years by the 3rd XV. In other words, they wished to play rugby with their friends.

Because most weeks there was a small overall surplus of players available, the committee introduced a scheme whereby players took it in turns to 'stand down'. Members tried their best to avoid their turn to miss playing.

The best-remembered case is Charles Barker's ploy. A senior member of the 3rd XV, he was the proprietor of a successful building company and employed young John Weston, also a regular member of the team. On several occasions, John Weston was forced to drop out of the 3rd XV because his boss, Charles Barker, needed him to work overtime for the whole of Saturday.

Halfway through the season, I realised that on each occasion John had telephoned me, apologising for not being able to play, it had been Charles Barker's turn to stand down. Charles would telephone later to ask, casually, whether there was any chance of a game on the Saturday. Relieved at a problem immediately solved, of course, I had always said yes.

I mentioned to the Prof my suspicions that Charles Barker was avoiding missing his Saturday rugby stand-down at John Weston's expense and asked if I should I put a stop to Charles' conduct. The Prof said, 'In my opinion, there are few opportunities in life to spread a little happiness. It would be prudent for you to put your suspicions out of your mind. John is young, hoping soon to marry, and no doubt welcomes the opportunity of working an extra day at overtime rates. Charlie Barker is most happy that he will be playing rugby on Saturday, and your good self will not be required to suffer the embarrassment of having to take the matter up with Charlie.' The subterfuge was allowed to continue.

The most surprising excuse for being unable to play was from a member of the selection committee present on the Monday evening, who, early Tuesday morning, telephoned me to apologise for now being unable to play on the Saturday. When he had returned home on the Monday evening, his wife had reminded him that she was expecting their first baby that Saturday, and, as she was having the baby at home, the midwife needed someone to provide plenty of hot water.

The full-back position was most unpopular and difficult to fill in the 3rd XV because missed tackles and other failures in this position were readily apparent, usually resulting in points for the opposition. Often, unable to persuade any member to fill that position, I had to be the reluctant 'last line of defence'.

In those days, forwards were allowed to dribble the ball at their feet. The accepted defensive ploy was for a defender to 'fall on the ball', placing his body between the ball and the attacking players. His team would then try to 'heel' the ball to regain possession.

There was terrified me, alone and facing three or four burly opposition forwards who were wearing leather boots with solid studs and bearing down on me, when, from nowhere, someone flashed past me and threw himself on the ball. I was saved from serious, if not fatal, injury, to my grateful thanks and relief.

In the bar after the match, I was describing the incident. As I hadn't recognised my saviour, I asked who he was and was told that he was a last-minute replacement for a player who had had to drop out. My informant then said, 'That sounds like Tony Reynolds. Did you notice that one of his arms is shorter than the other?' I hadn't.

He then related the following story: Tony, a member of the rugby club before the Great War, had risen to the rank of major, been awarded the MC and been wounded. Tony having been demobilised, his civilian career required him to leave the area. His mother continued to live in the village and Tony would periodically visit her at weekends, taking the opportunity on the Saturday morning to enjoy a few beers with pre-war friends at the rugby club.

It was on one of those visits that he called at the rugby club and, over a few beers, learned that three-quarters of an hour before kick-off the 3rd XV were still one player short.

On the spur of the moment, he said, 'I'll play,' and, before anyone could dissuade him, dashed off to his mother's house where his rugby kit was still sitting in a drawer in what had been, before the war, his room. He returned to the club in time to change and be ready to play minutes before the match began.

Tony's wife had forbidden him, on pain of divorce, to play rugby again. This Saturday would be his positively final match. An emotional occasion.

Having been told that Tony had been awarded the MC, I realised that his fearless performance on the rugby field made sense. During the war he and his platoon had become trapped in a slit trench which had come under continuous fire from a German machine-gunner. He and his men could neither advance nor retreat and four of his platoon had already been wounded.

Not known for having a patient disposition, he suddenly shouted, 'I'll sort the buggers out!', grabbed three grenades, climbed out of the trench and dashed towards the German machine-gunner. A low hedge gave him slight cover. He lobbed two of the grenades on to the target, silencing the firing from the machine-gun. Having extracted the pin from the third, he dropped the grenade, picked it up and, just to make sure, threw that as well. Unfortunately, because of the slight delay in throwing, the grenade went off soon after it left his hand. Although Tony was not injured, the blast from the explosion blew off his cap, which he began searching for amongst the mud, shell-holes and debris, much to the consternation of his platoon who were peeping over the edge of the trench, desperately trying to will him to leave the fucking cap and return to the comparative safety of the trench.

Having found his cap he began running back, but, before he reached the trench, he was hit in the right arm by a sniper's bullet. He was able to reach the trench, where his arm was bandaged, and he then led his platoon to a new position before making for the field hospital. Tony was awarded an immediate MC.

One of those at the bar listening to the narrative asked, 'What is an "immediate" MC? Do you mean to tell me that a general, or some other military bigwig, happened to be passing by, witnessed what Tony did and, forthwith, pulled from his pocket an MC, saying, "That was awfully brave; jolly good show! Here you are, my good fellow: an immediate MC, with my compliments? Great example to the men, don't you know"?'

The Prof, grateful for the opportunity to express his views, said, 'I am sure that you will all agree with me that it is tasteless for us to ridicule the actions of a very brave man. It seems to me that in this case, "immediate" meant that Tony would be awarded an MC without any delay or additional evidence.'

None of the Prof's audience knew whether or not his view was correct, but what he had said certainly subdued those present.

Pity about the deficiency in the arm department. A player like Tony would have been ideal (and very welcome) to replace me at full-back. Someone said, unkindly, that a full-back without any arms would be better than me. Of course, he had been drinking – well, I assume that he had.

JIM LAMBERT – OPERA CONVERT

Jim Lambert had two passions: the rugby club 3rd XV and Felicity Howard. He was quite content to languish in the rugby club 3rd XV; some members of the 3rd XV said that with his playing abilities it was just as well. His attitude to Felicity was quite different. He was ardent and resolute in his efforts to capture her affections.

Jim was good looking, still boyish with a straight nose, a firm jaw and a mass of unruly fair hair. At six feet in height he appeared to be slimmer than his measurements recorded.

Because he had done well in the mathematics papers of the exams he had taken before leaving school, his parents had decided that he should qualify as a chartered accountant. To do this he would need to be articled to a firm of chartered accountants for five years, receiving a nominal salary of one pound per week only in the fifth year. The limited allowance he received from his father was barely adequate. He continually had to choose between making the expected contributions to the social activities of the 3rd XV and financing his dedicated pursuit of Felicity. Not an easy choice.

Felicity was attractive, with dark brown hair and eyes to match. She was several inches shorter than Jim. She often wore a skirt and tight-fitting jumper, both coal black, which emphasised the contours of her slender and elegant figure. As Billyoddsocks said, 'Put a black beak in her mouth and she would make a very good crow.' Felicity was a talented musician, playing the clarinet in the local semi-professional orchestra; she particularly enjoyed opera. Early in her friendship with Jim she let it be known that she was not, as wives of rugby club members were expected to be, enthusiastic about doing the rugby club teas.

Felicity lived two miles from the town Her parents, both dead, had been diplomats, and she had been brought up for most of her life by two spinster great-aunts, all three being looked after by a resident housekeeper. There was, therefore, no walking Felicity home, the traditional method of enhancing a relationship.

Instead, taxis being expensive, the alternative was to join the queue in town for the last bus which stopped near Felicity's house. Any couple indulging in tender farewells were liable to be ridiculed, particularly on Saturday evenings, when the queue included boisterous individuals straight from the local pub. Although the bus stopped close to Felicity's house, Jim couldn't leave the bus to escort her to the front door because the bus returned to town by a different route.

Jim consoled himself with the thought that summer was imminent and Felicity and he could cycle to a secluded spot, concealed amongst trees, which he had frequented with a previous girlfriend.

Then it occurred to him: how would he explain to Felicity how he had discovered such a place?

Jim's problem was solved when he was surprised and delighted to learn that a godfather had bequeathed him 100 pounds, a sum sufficient to allow him to do three things: to celebrate his good fortune with his 3rd XV team-mates, to purchase a motorbike and, most importantly, to raise his entertaining of Felicity to a higher standard, even to the point of lavishness.

Jim suspected that his guardian angel was at last active on his behalf when it was announced in the local newspaper that a touring opera company would be visiting the local theatre, presenting an opera by Mozart. What an opportunity! He could take Felicity to the first-night charity performance, dinner before or supper afterwards – or why not both? The best seats, front row of the circle, end seats, as his father had always recommended, just in case there was a fire. He hoped that his initiative and the occasion would convince Felicity that he did really appreciate opera. It would not be easy because, before he had become aware of her obsession with opera, he had said to her that he could not tolerate opera because the plots were puerile, it was not possible to understand the words of the singers, it was difficult to determine who were the goodies and the baddies, and, anyway, operas were often in a foreign language.

Jim formally invited Felicity to the first-night charity performance. Felicity, surprised that Jim was willing to sit through a whole opera, graciously accepted the invitation with thanks and asked, 'What are we seeing?'

Jim replied, casually, 'Oh, it's Mozart.'

As soon as the box office opened, Jim purchased two tickets and made a reservation for dinner at the most fashionable local restaurant.

Leaving nothing to chance in impressing Felicity, Jim called at the local library to consult a book in order to familiarise himself with Mozart's opera. He checked the catalogue, and there it was in Gladys Davidson's book, *Standard Stories from the Operas*: an opera by Mozart. In his diary, Jim made a brief summary of the plot.

His ultimate worry was: would the new motorbike arrive in time for him to collect Felicity from her home? On past dates, lacking transport, Jim had always met Felicity in town. To now be in a position to collect her from her home on his brand new motorbike must surely impress her.

Great relief. The motorbike was delivered the day before the performance. The following day, Jim arrived on his motorbike at the address provided by Felicity, to discover that she lived in a large, rambling, Victorian house. He parked his motorbike on the grass verge outside the front gate, walked up the short drive and knocked on the door. This was opened by an elderly lady who held the door half-open, hesitating between prudence and courtesy. Felicity suddenly appeared, saying, 'It's for me, Auntie,' and then took Jim by his arm. Both of them walked down the front garden to where Felicity came face to face with Jim's sparkling new motorbike. Jim was gratified to note that Felicity was much impressed.

Jim mounted the bike and invited Felicity to sit on the pillion seat. He switched on the ignition, the bike jerked forward, and Felicity, unceremoniously, slid off the pillion on to the grass verge. As it was the first time she had sat on the pillion of a motorbike, she had not realised that she should grasp the body of the driver, and Jim, not yet familiar with the controls of his motorbike, had over-pressed the accelerator. Jim, always the gentleman, helped Felicity to her feet whilst gallantly offering to examine her nether regions to check whether or not there was any lasting damage, but Felicity insisted there wasn't and declined his thoughtful offer. Not a good start to Jim's ambitious plan.

Felicity and Jim arrived safely at the restaurant. During the meal, Jim led the conversation to the subject of the opera and, hoping to further impress Felicity, casually began outlining the plot of the Mozart opera: 'There are these two soldiers in Naples who were persuaded by a mutual friend to put their respective betrothed ladies through a test to confirm their fidelity...'

At the end of Jim's discourse, Felicity said, 'That's not what we are seeing. That's Mozart's *Cosi Fan Tutte*; we are seeing his *Magic Flute*.'

All Jim could say was, 'Ah.'

How was he to know Mozart wrote more than one opera?

88

After a most agreeable dinner and a bottle of wine, Felicity and Jim strolled to the theatre, arriving in good time. Jim purchased a programme, made sure that Felicity was seated comfortably and then said, 'Excuse me for a few minutes.'

When he returned from the Gents' and sat down, he realised that he had not zipped up his trousers. He bent over, intending to give the zip a surreptitious but determined pull. As he did so, both the ends of his tie became caught in the zip, preventing him from sitting upright. Several further attempts were unsuccessful. He had no alternative but to whisper to Felicity what had happened and tell her that he would have to visit the Gents' again to sort out the problem.

Walking bent over up the aisle to the rear of the theatre, he heard someone say, 'Oh, look! They are doing *The Hunchback of Notre Dame!*'

Arriving at the Gents' and unable to find a penny amongst the small change in his pocket, he had to persuade a fellow customer to change a sixpence. Several others in the Gents' viewed Jim with suspicion.

The opening handle was two thirds of the way up the door of the cubicle, and so, being bent over, he could not see where the slot for inserting the penny was placed. Only by his raising one arm and waving it around could his hand locate the slot. After dropping the penny twice, he finally gained entrance to the cubicle, pulled the tie over his head and removed his trousers, but he was able to release only one end of the tie from the zip.

Pressed for time, he decided to bundle up the tie and conceal it in the front of his trousers. At least he could now stand or sit upright.

Just before the curtain went up, Jim was able to return to his seat and tell Felicity what had happened. She began shaking. Jim, concerned, said, 'You are quivering; are you all right?'

She replied, 'Yes, I'm all right, if I could only stop laughing.'

So at the charity performance of Mozart's *Magic Flute*, amongst the Great and Good of the town, the ladies in their finery and the gentlemen wearing dark suits, there was one man in the front row of the circle wearing an open-necked shirt and with a suggestive bulge in the front of his trousers.

Despite Jim's conduct, he succeeded in his objective of impressing Felicity. She claimed that it was as a result of these events that she decided to marry Jim, because it was obvious that he desperately needed to be looked after by someone.

GERRY'S ROMANCE

Gerry Watson, one of the younger members of the 3rd XV, was afflicted from birth with a speech impediment. Despite this, Gerry had little difficulty in communicating with his friends, who soon became accustomed to his way of speaking; neither did it hamper his determined efforts to marry his girlfriend, Esmeralda. It was generally expected that they would soon fix a date.

Gerry was appalled and a little puzzled why, after over two years of friendship and courting, Esmeralda began failing to answer telephone calls, and generally putting him off when he suggested a date.

Via the 3rd XV grapevine Gerry soon learned that Esmeralda was being pursued with the aid of a two-litre Riley tourer by Tommy Bates, a well-known philanderer and ladies' man. Gerry couldn't understand why she was behaving in this manner.

Inexperienced in matters of the heart, Gerry decided to call on Billyoddsocks, a father figure of the 3rd XV, to confide in and ask what he should do to revive his relationship with Esmeralda.

'Billy,' he began, 'I do not know what's going on; I need some advice.'

Billy asked, facetiously, 'What's the matter? Are you changing sex?'

Gerry, ignoring the question, briefed Billy about Esmeralda and Tommy Bates. Billy's advice to Gerry was that the next time he happened to see Esmeralda he should tell her what sort of man Tommy Bates was; Gerry was doubtful, saying, 'She'll never believe me. In any case, I cannot do that; she lives the other side of the town and works shifts as a nurse in the Accident and Emergency department at the hospital. I am never likely to meet her accidentally.'

'Why don't you write her a letter?'

'I can't do that; Tommy Bates might sue me for libel.'

'Send her an anonymous letter.'

'No, she's bound to recognise my writing.'

Billyoddsocks, becoming aggravated, said, 'I know what you could do. Cut the words you want to use in the letter out of a newspaper or magazine, paste them on a piece of paper and post that.'

Much to Billyoddsocks' relief, Gerry agreed.

The next time Billyoddsocks met Gerry, he asked him if he had sent the letter to Esmeralda. Gerry's reply was, 'Well, not exactly, because I felt the letter wasn't strong enough. I had to describe Tommy as a first-class bounder, because I couldn't find the word I really needed in any newspaper or magazine.'

Billyoddsocks, ever resourceful, said, 'I've got a better idea. Why don't you visit the A&E department of the hospital? You might bump into Esmeralda, accidentally, of course.'

Gerry replied, 'She works shifts. How would I know when she was on duty?'

'Telephone beforehand and ask to speak to Nurse Esmeralda Green.'

'I don't know the number.'

Billyoddsocks, becoming exasperated, went to his desk, consulted his telephone directory and read out the number to Gerry. He pushed the telephone into Gerry's hand, saying, sharply, 'Get on with it... *now*!'

'Supposing she answers the telephone?'

Billyoddsocks sighed, then said, 'Slam it down.' He began mouthing the number, and Gerry meekly followed Billyoddsocks's lips as he dialled it.

Gerry was startled when the telephone rang and was answered almost instantaneously: 'Accident and Emergency.'

Gerry, after a few ums and ahs, carefully enunciated, slowly and as clearly as his impediment allowed, 'May I speak to Nurse Green?'

The reply was crisp. 'I'm afraid not. She will not be on duty again until she begins her shift at three o'clock tomorrow. Who shall I say called?'

Unprepared and flummoxed, Gerry said 'Syd.'

'Syd who?'

'Just say Syd. She'll know.'

Billyoddsocks, who had followed the gist of the conversation, congratulated Gerry, saying, 'There you are. Now all you have to do is go to the department tomorrow at about four o'clock and keep your eyes open for Esmeralda.'

Gerry asked, 'But what do I say if someone asks me what I am doing there?'

'Oh, tell them that you are expecting a headache.' Then, 'No, on second thoughts, explain that you have heard about a new treatment for your speech problem. They'll understand.'

'I have always been told that there is no cure for that. In any case, I am sure that I cannot just turn up at A&E. My GP must make an appointment for me with a consultant.'

Billyoddsocks, by now having exhausted his patience and really irritated, said, 'Just go to the bloody hospital tomorrow and see what happens.'

Gerry did just that.

On arrival at the Accident and Emergency department, Gerry joined a small queue at the admissions section. He was required to provide the usual basic details before being directed to a waiting area, where he spent the time thoroughly scrutinising every nurse who passed by. No Esmeralda.

Hearing his name called, he instinctively stood up to find at his elbow a gentleman in a white coat with a stethoscope dangling from his neck, who said, 'I am Dr Brennan. Please follow me.'

Dr Brennan' s surgery was crammed full with the tools of a doctor's trade: weighing machine, two gas bottles, trays of bandages and specimen bottles, a large stretcher surrounded by half-open curtains, a sinister-looking machine on a trolley with wires hanging down. One end of the surgery was curtained off.

On Dr Brennan's desk were two enormous piles of decrepit, frayed files, from which he selected a thin one, saying to Gerry, 'The last entry in your file was made when you had mumps about 14 years ago. I trust that you made a complete recovery?' He smiled at what he regarded as a joke intended to put his obviously perturbed patient at ease.

Gerry nodded, remembering the acute embarrassment he had endured in the school changing rooms after physical training.

Dr Brennan continued, 'I noticed in your file that you were born with a speech impediment. Has your ability to speak deteriorated or improved?'

Gerry replied that it was about the same, but immediately took the opportunity to say that he had come to the A&E because he had heard that there was now a more advanced treatment for his problem.

Dr Brennan patiently pointed out that the department, as its name implied, dealt solely with accidents and emergencies.

Seeing how crestfallen Gerry had become and taking pity on him, Dr Brennan continued, 'As you are here, I might as well tell you: there is a new treatment. It involves an operation on the roof of the mouth and you would be in hospital for about four days.

Gerry asked, 'How would I eat?'

'You would be fed by giving you a nutrient enema.'

'A nutrient enema? What is that?'

Dr Brennan explained that it was the anal method of supplying sustenance.

Gradually, the meaning of what Dr Brennan was saying dawned on Gerry. 'You mean up my... 'ere...?'

'Yes, exactly; up your 'ere'

'Will it hurt?'

'No, not at all.' Then, as he could see that Gerry was sceptical, he continued, 'It is about four o'clock, and my nurse is just about to bring in the tea. If you wish, I will ask her to give you a cup of tea by nutrient enema so that you can be satisfied that it is quite painless.'

The nurse with the tea tray entered the surgery. Dr Brennan asked her to give Gerry an enema, and, turning to Gerry, told him to go with the nurse behind the curtain at the end of the surgery and to remove his trousers.

Gerry did so and the nurse proceeded. Immediately, there were shouts from Gerry: 'Oh dear, oh dear, oh dear!'

Dr Brennan, alarmed, called out, 'What's the matter? What's the matter? Does it hurt?'

To which Gerry replied, 'No, no, I don't take sugar.'

As soon as Gerry's ordeal was over and he was restored to his trousers, with a hurried, 'Thank you, Doctor,' he scurried to the exit, not bothering to check whether any one of the passing nurses was Esmeralda.

On the way home, Gerry called on Billyoddsocks and gave him a blow-by-blow account of his visit to the A&E department. Congratulating Gerry on his performance,

Billyoddsocks was, for once, unable to proffer any further advice or suggestions to him. He was relieved when Gerry willingly informed him that he had decided to have the operation and, for the time being, to forget Esmeralda.

Gerry's local GP arranged an appointment with a consultant at the hospital, and a date was fixed for the operation. It was a complete success.

The day following, Gerry was dozing in hospital when he was disturbed by a nurse standing at the foot of his bed. It was Esmeralda.

She whispered, 'I am not supposed to be here, but I heard that you were in hospital. How are you? I can't stay long.'

Gerry was dumbfounded but managed to say that he was feeling better than he had expected. Esmeralda said, 'Good. Your speech seems to be much better. I'll try to pop in tomorrow,' and was gone.

During the next few days, Esmeralda made more surreptitious and fleeting visits. The day before Gerry was to be discharged, as she was opening the door to leave, she half-turned and said, 'Oh, by the way, I haven't seen Tommy Bates for ages,' and disappeared.

After he left the hospital, Gerry lost no time in contacting Esmeralda.

The flames of love were rekindled, wedding bells tolled, and, as all virtuous tales should end, all was well.

Actually, not quite all.

Esmeralda's tea-brewing abilities and sandwich-making skills were just not quite up to the high standards to which the 3rd XV had become accustomed.

EGERTON LANCELOT JOHNSON

Egerton L Johnson, or 'Eggie', always treated me with great kindness and respect because I was one of the few people who knew that the 'L' stood for 'Lancelot', a fact that he preferred should not become widely known to the public in general and his fellow members of the 3rd XV in particular.

He was without question the most ardent member of the club, never missing a match, training or a club social event. His rugby-playing skills were at best somewhat limited because, as he said, without his glasses he never knew quite where the ball was. He always turned up fully kitted out, ready to play whether or not he had been selected. The only Saturdays he would be absent were when he had acquired a ticket for an international at Twickenham. Even then, he rushed back to be in time for a few pints in the rugby club.

At an early age, Eggie showed that he had a talent for writing, and so he became regarded as the rugby club bard. He published his work in his early teens, but unfortunately, as will become apparent, these early efforts and subsequent contributions to literature failed to survive and were lost to posterity.

Eggie's literary career centred around the rugby club, which used as its headquarters two converted barns adjoining the Rose & Crown, facing the pitch. Club members and supporters were permitted to use the pub's facilities, and it was in the Gents' that Eggie's literary talents were first exposed to the critical world. He covered the walls of the urinals with such traditional gems as:

No matter how you strive and strain, the last drop down your leg will drain.

Please do not put cigarette butts in the urinals as it makes them damp and difficult to light.

Where'er ye be let wind be free; church or chapel, let it rattle.

Plus regular pointed observations on current events, local politics, Arsenal, the meaning of life in three instalments, advice to those about to marry and seasonal greetings. '*Merry Xmas to all my readers*' usually remained until just before Easter, when Eggie crossed out '*Xmas*' and merely substituted '*Easter*'.

Poetry was not Eggie's strong point. One of his quotes was:

Stands the clock at ten past three and is there still kippers for tea? (Herbert Cook's Godmanchester)

In the visitors' changing room he put up a notice:

3rd XV's results to date

Won	the toss four times
Lost	two balls
Drew	blood eight times

Sadly, some years later that area of the Rose & Crown was refurbished and Eggie's literary works were lost, forever submerged by four coats of Dulux.

Eggie was the progeny of the Great and Good of the nearby town. His father had inherited a large furniture store and his mother two chemist's shops. As he was the only child of the marriage, an agreeable and comfortable life for Eggie appeared to be assured.

Each of his parents harboured hopes that Eggie would choose one or both businesses as a career and perpetuate the family name. They agreed that neither would endeavour to influence the choice of their son in any way.

As Eggie progressed through school it became obvious that he was somewhat eccentric. He was just under six feet tall, his head covered with a mass of disobedient black curly hair. He wore black-rimmed bifocal glasses which magnified his eyes, giving the impression that they were too large for his face. He was most comfortable wearing a sleeveless shirt and dark casual trousers held up by a wide black belt with a large brass buckle. Tennis shoes were his preferred footwear. Not the appropriate attire for a future owner of a furniture emporium or a qualified chemist. He had no ambitions for any particular career.

Not surprisingly, when he finally left school, much to the disappointment of his parents, Eggie was not interested in joining either of the family businesses. Conscious of his family obligations and to pacify his parents, however, he offered to work six months in each business before he made any decision about his future career. His parents were greatly relieved that there was still hope that Eggie might join one or the other of the businesses.

For his first work experience, Eggie turned up at the furniture emporium, uncomfortably attired in a white shirt and stiff collar with an appropriate sombre tie, dark suit and sensible shoes, to learn the art of chatting up and persuading reluctant customers to purchase beds and three-piece suites.

For mental stimulation Eggie attended evening classes in French, a language in which he had acquired a grounding at school. When holiday time arrived, his parents, ever anxious to please their son, offered to pay for him to spend a week in Paris.

Eggie's mother swung into action to ensure that during his visit to Paris nothing untoward should happen to her beloved son, because, as she said, 'Paris is full of foreigners and you cannot be too careful.'

His luggage included a complete change of underwear and a selection of pills and potions to cure any foreign ailments he might contract, plus a special pill to 'keep him regular'. He was earnestly advised not to drink the water, and in no circumstances to engage in conversation with any attractive French lady walking down the street, leading a dog.

Eggie thoroughly enjoyed his visit to Paris. After his return he was in the rugby club bar, recounting his adventures in Paris to a group of members. One of these adventures had puzzled him.

Pressed to explain what he meant, he said, 'I was sitting in this café, which was very busy. I had just ordered a coffee when I saw a very pretty girl enter the cafe; she looked around and realised that every table was occupied. Then, seeing me sitting alone at a table, she came straight over, smiled at me, and sat down opposite me, still smiling. After a few minutes, she rummaged in her handbag, took out a pencil and drew on the back of the menu a bed.'

Eggie's audience became agog with expectation, their imaginations running wild. Eggie continued, 'What puzzles me is, how did she know that I am in the furniture business?'

I admired those listening because none of them laughed, most instead murmuring, 'Yes, Eggie, very puzzling, very puzzling indeed.'

After the agreed period in the furniture business, Eggie arrived at the main chemist's shop to begin the six-month trial period. Wearing the same uncomfortable suit, he gradually began to learn how to deal with customers needing medical items.

He was perplexed when young lads came into the shop and asked for 'a packet of three'. Eggie would ask, 'Three what?' and the lads, embarrassed, would say, 'Toothbrushes.' Eggie couldn't understand why anyone, let alone a young lad, would need three toothbrushes.

On one occasion, a very attractive foreign-looking lady with a very small dog on a long lead came into the shop and asked, 'Do you have anything for getting rid of unwanted hair?'

Eggie replied, 'Yes, we have an excellent ointment; you rub it in thoroughly under your arms and in three days the unwanted hair has gone. It never fails.'

The lady said, 'Actually, it is not for under my arms; it is for my Chihuahua.'

Eggie quickly said, 'In that case, rub it in carefully in exactly the same way but do not ride a bicycle for three days.'

Still undecided about his future, Eggie lingered on in the family chemist's shop only to learn that his mother had been diagnosed with inoperable cancer. She died three months later. Worse was to follow when, shortly after her death, his father suffered a fatal heart attack.

Eggie was now the sole owner of two profitable businesses and a large family house. He was a rich man.

Eggie lost no time in selling both businesses and the family home. From the proceeds he put a few thousand pounds aside, as he put it, 'to use as petty cash'. The remainder he invested in a life annuity, claiming, 'I'll never have to work again.'

He left the area and moved to London, rented a flat and, using his petty cash, embarked on a hedonistic lifestyle which was only curtailed by the outbreak of war in September 1939. For a few months, on a Saturday evening, he would turn up in the village and enjoy a pint or two in the rugby club.

After he was called up for military service, he completely lost touch with the village and the rugby club.

Nearly 60 years later, I was attending a wedding in Sarzora in Goa. Walking down the village street I noticed a man sitting on the veranda of a house, reading what appeared to be a copy of the Overseas Weekly Telegraph. His tousled grey hair and thick, black-rimmed glasses reminded me of Eggie.

Impossible.

Intrigued, I walked up the short entrance drive and asked, 'Is your name, by any chance, Eggerton Johnson?'

He looked up, gazed at me for a minute or two, put down the newspaper, then said, 'Who wants to know?'

Before I could answer, he stood up, ordered me to 'Stay there' and disappeared into the house. He soon returned and threw something at me which, instinctively, I caught. It was an old, partly deflated rugby ball, leather covered and well worn, with the original stitches still in place.

My original question did not now require a reply.

He produced a bottle of feni (Goan firewater) and two glasses, and invited me to join him on the veranda. After a few drinks had loosened his tongue, I encouraged him to tell me what he had been doing since we had last met.

He was called up in 1940 and spent nearly five years in the army, in which period, he claimed, he never heard a shot fired in anger and spent most of his time well behind the front line, washing his white flag to ensure that it was always clean and bright, just in case.

Returning to civilian life, he realised that the purchasing power of his annuity had, since 1939, dramatically decreased. His pre-war hope that he would never have to work again could not now be realised.

He took a variety of jobs, one of which was that of a long-distance lorry driver. In the late 1950s he was assigned to the London–Lisbon route.

At that time, Portugal still possessed Goa. As a marketing ploy, the Portuguese International Airline scoured Goa for the most attractive girls to act as air-hostesses. Clothed in white saris, they were known as the 'Doves of India' and caused a sensation in Lisbon every time they arrived from Goa.

Eggie met one of these girls, Teresa, when she was in Lisbon resting before the return flight to Goa. They spent the day together, planning to meet again the next time Teresa was in Lisbon; Eggie, by chatting up the girl in his office, managed to arrange for his next trip to coincide with her stopover there. This arrangement, with the occasional hiccough, continued for several weeks; they became close and decided to marry.

Teresa introduced Eggie to two of her brothers who resided in Lisbon; both gave Teresa their blessing, and Eggie was invited to visit Goa to obtain the formal permission of Teresa's family.

The next time Teresa made the trip, Eggie returned with her on the same plane. He was presented to the family and unanimously approved.

Eggie liked what he saw of Goa. On his return to England, he resigned from the transport company, and after seemingly endless bureaucratic delays, Teresa and Eggie were married in a Catholic church in Lisbon.

The family into which Eggie had married was not large by Portuguese/Indian standards. Teresa had three brothers, two residing in Lisbon and the third living in Bombay, plus three unmarried sisters still at home, the youngest in her final year at school.

Teresa's father owned the rambling family house, situated in about two hectares. It was surrounded by a spacious covered veranda and, except for the chimney breasts, built entirely of wood. Most of the land produced sufficient income from growing cashew nuts to enable him to educate his children and enjoy a reasonable standard of living. Part of the land was a cultivated market garden to which Teresa's father tended, adequately providing for the family's needs.

Teresa and Eggie moved in to the family house. Teresa continued as an air-hostess on a reduced schedule and Eggie occasionally pottered around helping Teresa's father in the market garden.

Although Eggie still received a pittance from his annuity he realised that if he and Teresa wanted to raise a family they would have to find or purchase a house for themselves, because the family house was full to capacity already. Not only would they have to find alternative accommodation, but Eggie would have to find a source of income to replace Teresa's salary as an air-hostess.

Eggie's desire never to have to work again would have to be put on hold.

Eggie cashed in his annuity and used the proceeds to purchase a site for a property. He found a sizable plot, and, by crossing the right palms with rupees, permission to build a house was obtained.

The necessity to leave the family house became less urgent when Teresa's two elder sisters announced that they would be marrying in the near future. Eggie did not hurry to begin building the house.

About this time Eggie met two local entrepreneurs who were offering to sell plots overlooking the beach on the nearby coast for development. Eggie came to an arrangement with them that he would exploit mainly the British market, receiving a generous commission on the sales that he concluded.

Eggie drafted advertisements and, by post, placed them in the press in Britain and Bombay. The response was immediate and well beyond his expectations. He sold many plots, receiving deposits which he passed on to the entrepreneurs. With the property boom in Goa not showing any signs of abating, Eggie began to feel confident that he would never have to work again.

Both his disbursements and the commission due to him mounted rapidly. When he asked the entrepreneurs for a substantial payment on account, they prevaricated. Losing his patience, he visited their offices in Margão; he was horrified to find that the offices were devoid of furniture and the whereabouts of the two entrepreneurs unknown. Further enquiries revealed that they had no legal ownership of the properties which they were purporting to sell.

Eggie realised with alarm that he was personally liable to these buyers because he had issued receipts in his own name for their deposits.

The deceived investors both in Britain and Goa reported their losses to the appropriate authorities, and Eggie became, as he put it, 'a wanted man on two continents'.

Playing for time, Eggie ignored letters from Britain. In Goa, he made use of an old local custom by acquiring, at a small fee, the services of the clerk in charge of scheduling criminal cases. The case against him never came to court because every time Eggie's case reached the top of the pile of cases due for hearing, the clerk replaced the file at the bottom of the pile.

The property boom in Goa had attracted immigrants from other parts of India, placing a heavy strain on the infrastructure, particularly with the need for schools. The local authority decided that the land on which Teresa and Eggie were proposing to build their house, on the outskirts of the village, would be an ideal location for a new school. Thousands of rupees changed hands, providing Eggie and Teresa with a considerable capital profit.

I interjected, 'So, I suppose you were able to say, "I'll never have to work again."'

Eggie said, 'No, no, not at all. You are wrong. I tracked down the investors who lost money on the land scam and reimbursed them, so I am in the clear.'

I pointed out that the fact that the investors had been reimbursed did not necessarily absolve him of his responsibility for his original crime.

'Now you tell me,' Eggie said.

I asked him, 'Do you ever visit the UK?'

He replied, 'No, not at all. For some time after the property deal went sour I was too frightened that there might be an armed policeman from Scotland Yard waiting in the arrivals section of Heathrow to greet me and clap a pair of handcuffs on me. In any case, I am more than content here in Goa amongst my five children, numerous in-laws and young grandchildren, nine at the last count.

'What made you bring a rugby ball to Goa?'

'I thought that I might be able to introduce the game here, but the Goans couldn't understand why the ball wasn't round. They thought that I was some sort of nutcase.'

'So can you now say, "I'll never have to work again"?'

'Not quite yet. After paying off the investors I needed a source of income to support my family. Luckily for me, an old man who had for years owned a cheap and cheerful café on the edge of the beach died. I managed to persuade his heirs to sell me the lease. I updated the café and added a section offering souvenirs of Goa and any items which would appeal to tourists for sale. It is a gold mine. No one in the family is interested in taking over the café, so I have just sold the business for a substantial sum. Completion will be in four weeks' time, then I'll never have to work again.

We reminisced for another hour or so until I (suffering from an overdose of feni) stood up to leave. Eggie said, 'Don't give my address to anyone, and don't you write to me because I shall not reply. There is nothing I want from the UK.'

I said, 'Oh, yes, there is; you certainly need a new rugby ball...'

He smiled.

A month after I returned from Goa, I received a letter from one of Teresa's brothers to advise me that just after the completion of the sale of the café, Eggie had, like his father before him, suffered a fatal stroke.

At last Eggie would never have to work again.

EPILOGUE

Relaxing here on the beach at Estoril, watching the sea trying to make up its mind whether to ebb or flow, I 'see' in my mind's eye those characters of the 3rd XV and I imagine that I can hear them in the bar telling stirring tales of their dazzling runs through bewildered defenders, fearless tackles which avoided defeat and penalties kicked from impossible distances.

Sadly, most of the participants in these remarkable events have been summoned by the Great Captain above to their last match in the sky, their voices forever stilled.

I miss them.

Very much.

AUTHOR'S PROFILE

d'Arcy Orders MBE is a graduate of Cambridge University and was much involved in reviving the Footlights Dramatic Club after the War, serving as the hands-on President for the first post-war Revues of 1947 and 1948.

Nice Try is his first attempt at humorous writing and, at 89, he describes himself as a Footlights Late Developer. He resides in Cambridge with his wife Susie.